Force.com for Everyone:

How to power your Customer Company with Smart Process Applications

Jonathan Sapir

Author of *Unleash the Power of Force.com* and *The Executives Guide to Force.com*

With Peter Fingar

Author of *dot.Cloud* and *Enterprise Cloud Computing*

Foreword by Peter Coffee

VP and Head of Platform Research at Salesforce

Books by Jonathan Sapir

Igniting the Phoenix
A new vision for IT (2003)

Power in the Cloud
Using cloud computing to build information systems at the edge of chaos (2009)

Unleash the power of Force.com
How to thrive in the new digital economy (2011)

The Executives Guide to Force.com
Enabling Shadow IT and Citizen Developers in the age of Cloud Computing (2012)

The Quick Start Guide to Implementing Force.com (2012)

Force.com for Everyone
How to power your Customer Company with Smart Process Applications (2013)

Smart Process Apps
The Next Breakout Business Advantage (2013)

Force.com 101
101 things you need to know about Force.com (2013)

Table of Contents

Preface

My interest in business users being able to develop their own applications dates back to my time at IBM in the early 1980's. In those days, the cloud was an IBM mainframe, and the end user tool was a language called APL. It was well ahead of its time, but it showed the enormous benefits that could be reaped from users building their own solutions without the need to involve IT.

A lot has happened since that time, with the introduction of spreadsheets and tools like MS Access aimed at non-technical users. But the ability for users to build powerful, scalable, maintainable solutions that can work across the enterprise has been elusive.

Until now.

With the advent of the cloud, one of the biggest barriers to serious user application development has been eliminated – infrastructure. The cloud eliminates the need for users to procure, install, upgrade and maintain hardware and software, and the need to performs backups and other operational functions.

Another major barrier to fall is the lack of "tech-savviness" on the part of users. This of course has changed dramatically, as Millennials become more dominant in the workplace. Having used computers almost all their lives, and having learned things like spreadsheet programming and databases in high school and college, the Millennial user is much more capable of taking things into their own hands without having to wait for IT.

A "smart process application builder" on a comprehensive platform like Force.com provides the framework within which end user computing can thrive. Smart process applications (SPA) lowers the barrier to entry, much like drones lower the barrier to entry for doing much of the work that a jet pilot with years of training and expertise would do.

SPA does this by eliminating the need to understand the most complex parts of application development – things like database modeling, application architecture, and all the support functionality every application requires, like security, permissions, performance, scalability, etc.

The advent of mobile has also made it a lot easier than before. Mobile requires the development of small, role-based, highly customized apps, not large, monolithic, generic solutions. It is much easier for users to conceptualize and build these small applications, and then use the capability of SPA to orchestrate them with the apps built by others, resulting in enterprise solutions that are easily implemented and modified.

This book provides an understanding of SPA and the Force.com platform, and why SPA is critical to every organization that wants to become what Salesforce calls a "Customer Company" – an enterprise completely dedicated to fulfill the unique needs of every customer.

The sooner your organization understands the overall power of Force.com and the potential of SPA, the faster you will be able to become an effective Customer Company!

Jonathan Sapir
CEO, SilverTree Systems, Inc.
www.silvertreesystems.com

Foreword: Simplicate and Add Cloudiness

By Peter Coffee, VP and Head of Platform Research, salesforce.com inc.

Several iconic engineers have been quoted as directing their apprentices, "simplicate and add lightness" – but the dictum was best elaborated by Lotus Cars founder Anthony Colin Bruce Chapman. As he explained, "Adding power makes you faster on the straights. Subtracting weight makes you faster everywhere." Welcome to a handbook of "faster everywhere" thought and action.

It seems obvious once you say it, and the oft-used airy metaphor of 'the cloud' seems like an obvious setup for a doctrine of "add lightness" – but it takes more than those two words to overcome decades of IT complexification.

In particular, people have struggled for decades to lighten and simplicate IT by getting rid of the middleman: by putting business technology closer to the people who are most directly accountable for meeting the business requirement. Too often, this comes from a profoundly negative opinion of those who devote their lives to IT practice.

Some of the business community's most influential thinkers have been downright confrontational in their comments on dedicated IT teams: Robert Townsend, in his breakthrough 1970 manifesto Up the Organization, warned against what he called "computers and their priests," saying that "Most of the computer technicians that you're likely to meet or hire are complicators, not simplifiers. They're trying to make it look tough. Not easy. They're building a mystique, a priesthood, their own mumbo-jumbo ritual to keep you from knowing what they—and you—are doing."

When IT gets tarred with the brush of "complicator, not simplifier," it's bad for everyone.

- It leads to a defensive mentality of "don't let IT run wild," instead of an innovative mentality of "let's see what this can do." Townsend, in fact, further warned of the need to "separate those who want to use their skills to help your company from those who just want to build their know-how on your payroll." That suspicion discourages investments in training, entrenching and calcifying practitioners in the skills that they already have – and impelling the most forward-looking to look elsewhere for advancement. This book may invite some re-thinking.

- It leads to a monument-builder behavior of gathering requirements for months before anything gets built at all — because it's assumed that whatever gets built will have to last for years, too inertial for iterative improvement, thanks to the combination of cumbersome technology and hoops-of-fire contracting practices. The people with the most to contribute — the most knowledge, the most energy, the most passion and purpose — will be the most likely to avoid entanglement in what Edward Yourdon famously called "Death March" projects. This book is about a means for their re-engagement by giving them more hope of prompt, accurate, and continuously improving satisfaction.

- **It absolutely does not lead to daring, market-leading enchantment of the customer driven by relentless focus on customer success**. Let's concentrate for a moment on this particular goal: fanatical obsession with success as defined by customers, not by vendors.

Peter Drucker wrote something in 1974 that I believe is too easy to misunderstand, when he wrote "There is only one valid definition of business purpose: *to create a customer*." [italics in original] I believe that too many people think of this in the vein of another famous quotation, "There's a sucker born every minute" (often but wrongly ascribed to P.T. Barnum; more likely spoken by his critic David Hannum).

I think people hear the phrase "create a customer" and think of it as meaning the conjuring of a desire with no underlying value, but that is absolutely not what Drucker had in mind. If we look at the paragraphs surrounding that Drucker quotation, we find a much more interesting statement of what every provider of services or goods is actually achieving: "The want a business satisfies may have been felt by the customer before he or she was offered the means of satisfying it. Like food in a famine, it may have dominated the customer's life and filled all his waking moments, but it remained a potential want until the action of businesspeople turned it into an effective demand. Only then is there a customer and a market."

Like Chapman, Drucker is saying something that's absolutely obvious once we hear it: I'm not a customer at all, until I'm offered a chance to make some payment for some need – that is, until I discover and enter a market. But "markets are not created by God, nature, or economic forces but by businesspeople," Drucker further observed, concluding "…it is business action that creates the customer."

This is a powerful, vision-changing statement. It means that we do not start a successful business by defining what we want to sell, then following up with a campaign to create a momentary state of customer willingness to pay for it (without concern for subsequent "buyer's remorse").

We should rather begin by looking for a void in the cosmos of markets, a region of economic space in which a need is not finding a market that offers opportunities to address it. Finding those voids is a pursuit that's driven by extensive knowledge of many different things: by experience with current customers, including both their frustrations and their delights, and by a mastery of many technologies that can tell the difference between incremental and transformative change.

This is why the role of the "knowledge worker," and the empowerment of knowledge workers to strengthen and accelerate their own contributions, must be forcefully communicated and achieved. We find Peter Drucker once again taking point, since he's generally credited with coining the phrase "knowledge worker" in 1959. Even so, there are Druckerisms on this subject that one might challenge – or clarify.

In particular, you'll find Drucker quoted in this very book as having said, "A knowledge worker is someone who knows more about his or her job than anyone else in the organization" – something he wrote almost forty years after first coining the label. Frankly, I suspect that Drucker made that statement as a warning to managers: an admonition that they needed to learn to coordinate the work of people who knew more than their supervisors about key subject matter in their jobs, which is not the traditional relationship of worker to boss.

I believe that Drucker meant this comment about "someone who knows more" to be descriptive, but not definitional – in the same way that a master woodworker might have a large collection of wood, as raw material for future projects, but it is not the size of the woodpile that makes the master. It's the ability to know which piece best suits the present need, and the ability to add value to it with confidence and speed. This book is all about giving the knowledge worker a better shop full of precision power tools.

There's another management viewpoint that's represented at many points in this book: the world as seen by Dilbert. Anyone who engages in modern business practice, and especially in business technology, has to seek a balance between Drucker's inspirations and Dilbert's warnings. Drucker offers a vision of why business exists, and how it can be made to serve that root purpose better than ever before; Dilbert offers a reminder of how easily it can all go terribly wrong.

If making things easy were enough, this book would not be needed. Using newly accessible power to do the right things, while avoiding expensive or even catastrophic rediscovery of the ways that technology can "speed up the mess" (as Townsend wrote), is what will make the investment of your time here worthwhile.

Peter Coffee
VP and Head of Platform Research
salesforce.com inc.

Smart Process Applications one year later

By Craig Le Clair, Forrester

There has been over 70% turnover for the Global Fortune G500 companies over the past 10 years. That's right. Seven out of ten companies have dropped off that list - unable to manage an accelerating pace of change that has brought – pervasive Internet connectivity, cloud-based applications, mobile devices that connect everywhere, information workers who use their own tools to do corporate work on their own time, and products built with 3D printers. Not exactly a news flash, but rapid change and digital disruption is here to stay. And this brings us to Smart Process Applications.

About a year ago, a group of Forrester analysts covering mobility, social, and Business Process trends starting seeing the emergence of a new software market. We characterized the last decade as a near obsession with software platform approaches like CRM, ERP, Data Warehouses that – much like the relative that stays too long –consumed budget, skills, and mindshare. These systems are the transactional backbone of most enterprise - but struggle to address "invisible" and untamed processes (those that cross departmental boundaries, involve humans, and weave in and out of core systems). But it's not their fault. They were designed for an era when companies could rely on a sustained competitive advantage with predictable and stable events, and not for the increasing volume of less predictable exceptions. For many enterprises 75% of their IT budgets are consumed by their care. This was not sustainable as the world was shifted to the "Age of the Customer" driven by mobile and social media trends.

We became convinced that something new had to emerge to close this gap, something that had a foot both in the new and old worlds. We called them Smart Process Apps — and forecasted the market as reaching $34 billion in 2015.

Breaking the SPA handle down is helpful; "Smart" means charged by advancing analytics; "Process" means –unlike most mobile apps today – they connect to core systems and the business and are fueled by the agility of BPM and Case Management, and "Apps" means that the process starts from a smart device or tablet. Smart process apps –– have caught the attention of business executives and the IT community.

And here's the real problem. Our workers have changed and so have our customers. Enterprises now need solutions that allow customers and workers to accomplish routine transactions on mobile devices – that are always connected and where process boundaries have been pushed out to the customer or to those serving the customer at the point of service. Fewer processes start at the company's firewall or with events received in the back office –where these systems shine.

SPAs emphasize social data, immediacy, context, and ease of use is to help companies re-establish a more human connection. In an ironic twist, our obsessive connectivity driven by consumer technology has led a greater dependency on technology, and less dependency on humans. A new form of isolation. And for years, process improvement efforts have automated processes to the point that people often are no longer involved. Many enterprises, taking this automation to an extreme, have created frustrating, bewildering islands of automation without any human touch for customers. Leading companies will soon differentiate on the personality and quality of a more personalized experience – and SPAs will play a role.

How do SPAs help? They float above but interact where needed with core systems. They are lighter, easier to change, assume mobile, and use big data and analytics to predict events and drive actions. And unlike mobile apps., they know how to integrate and leverage core systems. The Apple App. Store has thousands of business apps that are barely used. The main reason: they lack a process layer. They do not interact well with existing information and processes. So enter SPAs and a new era where focus – on a business domain and problem – leverage of core systems and processes, now trumps the promise of scope.

Introduction

We see our customers as invited guests to a party, and we are the hosts. It's our job to make the customer experience a little bit better.
– Jeff Bezos, Amazon.com CEO

Behind the scenes of any party you'll find an incredible amount of work going on. There are cooks, decorators, waiters, musicians – and all of them have to be coordinated, managed and staged. These players must also be capable of handling anything that might go wrong – a late delivery, broken glass, spoiled dessert – in such a way that the guests never even notice.

If the supporting cast fails in its responsibilities, your chances of hosting a successful party go right out the window, no matter how charming and gracious you are toward your guests.

This book is about ensuring a smooth experience for your customers so you can treat them like valued guests at an exclusive party, and thereby meet and exceed the expectations of each of them individually.

It's about laying the foundation for a Customer Company.

Customer	To become an effective Customer Company, everyone in your extended organization must work together in the interests of the customer.
force.com	They can only do this effectively if they are working off a common set of data and information, and are communicating and collaborating through a common medium.
	They must ensure that the entire organization and its partners can effectively be harnessed in unison to ensure the customer is provided with a smooth, customized and efficient experience. This requires an element of structure and control to ensure everyone knows what they need to do and when they need to do it, and to be able to respond efficiently when things go off track.

Becoming a Customer Company

Today's customers understand they now have power—and they know how to use it. They have expectations—and they have recourse if those expectations aren't met. They have a voice. And, it is loud and far-reaching and boundless. That's why earning customer loyalty now goes way beyond a loyalty program. You need to recognize them as more than just numbers or accounts, but as unique human beings with distinct sets of needs. You need to acknowledge that they now expect more than just a product or service. They expect a relationship that is on equal terms. You need to earn their trust.
  - Salesforce, *How to become a customer company*

Today we are in the midst of a customer revolution - customers are connected 24/7, and they are better informed and have more choices than ever before. There is a major shift in how people access information from the cloud and how they share it using social applications. There is also a shift in customers' expectations - they require a consistent experience anywhere they are, with any content, on any device.

In this new world, customer loyalty is the currency by which companies will live or die. More than ever before, customers are truly in charge.

They expect to be at the center of your world, and you need to put them there.

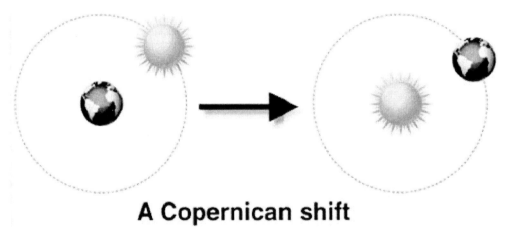

A Copernican shift

Figure 1: Instead of the customer conforming to the contours of the organization, the organization conforms to the needs of the customer.

It is easy commit to delivering great service, but how can you do this efficiently and effectively – every time, with every customer?

It starts with the frontline of the organization working directly with the customer, determining exactly what they need, and then leveraging the rest of the organization to get it done. The better any business can do this, the higher their customer satisfaction, and (most likely) the lower their costs as they optimize their responses. This is highly people-centric, using real-time data to create a solution or process to suit the circumstances.

> *.... Rather than ask what we are good at and what else we can do with that skill, you ask who are our customers? What do they need? And then you say we are going to give that to them regardless of whether we have the skills to do so...*
> - Jeff Bezos on "working backwards"

This requires working from the outside-in, rather than the inside-out.

Enterprise IT can be defined as "inside-out" since it starts from the back office, and is focused on activities "inside" the enterprise. There are only a few activities requiring access "outside," such as use of the Internet, and even for these, control is managed from the "inside."

In the back office, the environment is structured and optimized for maximum efficiency. By contrast, the front office is an unstructured, customer-facing operational area built around talented people who want access to real-time information to make the right business decision at the right time.

Trying to deliver this new outside world from the inside shows a failure to recognize that the enabling technology is radically different. The inside-out model of traditional IT is based on stable, large, monolithic enterprise applications using client-server technology. On the other hand, outside-in is based on rapidly changing, small, cloud-based services. Each and every important technology characteristic is exactly reversed, as is the purpose for which the business user or manager wants to use it[1]!

---

[1] Andy Mulholland, Capgemini Global Chief Technology Officer

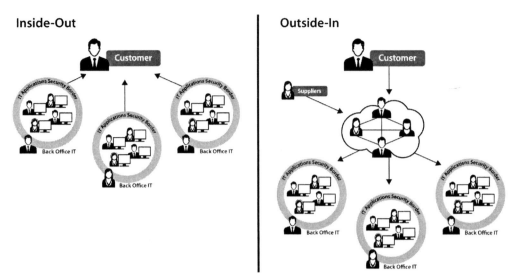

Figure 2: When working outside-in, each component of the organization interacts with the customer separately. This is fine when everything goes according to plan. But when it doesn't, resolving the problem requires the staff of each component to interact together in a unique way to suit each event.

The challenge exists around rapid and frequent introductions of new types of apps and services that allow interaction through social and collaborative tools. In adopting an outside-in approach, the relevant users and devices are moved outside the existing secure enterprise IT environment, permitting the loose-coupled, independent consumption of "services" on-demand that is the core of this new environment.

Outside-in is a completely different way of thinking about the requirement, delivery, and deployment model. But this is only to be expected, given that this is an entirely new generation of technologies used in a completely different way by businesses. This is just like the major shift in the early '90s when using PC network technology changed every aspect of the mini-computer requirement, delivery, and deployment model to the model we understand today as Enterprise IT.

Inside-Out	Outside-In
Starts by asking what the company can do with existing resources.	Starts by asking what the customer wants, regardless of existing resources.
Focuses on operational capabilities to make the organization more streamlined and efficient.	Focuses on empowering organizations to do business with the outside world.
Sees the new technology as an evolution of technology within the enterprise.	Sees the new technology as a new set of opportunities for delivering services and maximizing business opportunities.
The environment is inward-facing, structured, built around systems, and is as automated as possible.	The environment is customer-facing, unstructured, built around people who need access to information in real time to make the right decisions at the right time.
Monolithic enterprise applications support a centralized computing environment for efficiency.	Highly targeted, orchestrated-as-needed micro-applications support ultimate agility.
Requires line of business-independent decision making and local optimization.	Requires consistency, visibility, and effectiveness – from the customer's perspective.
Approaches the challenge of consistency via a horizontal, process-oriented approach that tries to break down organizational silos, in effect stifling agility.	Approaches the challenge of consistency by providing a layer of consistency that exists *outside* the individual silos, thereby providing both consistency and agility.
Changing back-office systems is hard and therefore relatively rare.	Change is a constant need.
Out-of-the-box solutions are common and appropriate.	Out-of-the-box solutions are usually inappropriate.
Focus on mass production.	Focus on mass customization.

Becoming an outside-in Customer Company requires an organization to[2]:

---

[2] Adapted from Salesforce, *How to become a customer company: Your guide to connecting customers, employees, partners, and products in a whole new way*

Provide a consistent user interface

Provide customers with a single, seamless point of integration with your organization, regardless of which application or process they are involved in.

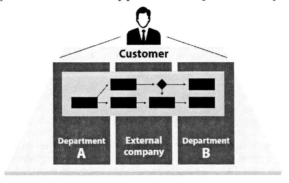

Build and deploy solutions quickly

The capabilities and limitations of existing applications cannot be used to constrain what can be built and how quickly they can be deployed. Highly customized business processes must be built, which include data and services currently locked inside your back-office systems.

Improve and innovate continuously

Improve and adapt your processes to keep up with your customers' evolving needs by quickly building and deploying solutions that engage customers with the right functionality and content, in the right place, at the right time. Innovation must be business-as-usual.

Create efficiencies

Get to market faster so you can gain a real competitive edge. Create efficiencies by quickly finding out what's working and what's not. Automate to gain more control of everything from routine discounts to product exceptions to proposals. Reduce errors, speed up workflows, and keep employees focused on adding real value.

Collaborate effectively

Get employees more informed, more in touch and more collaborative. As product experts, operators, and creative types rally around an activity, it puts everyone on the same page and knocks down blockers fast. Allow them to collaborate directly in the context of a business task. Add social feeds, comments, likes, groups, private messages, and recommendations to your business apps so employees can stay up to date and collaborate around customer records, documents, dashboards, etc.

Unlock your legacy data

Unlock the wealth of critical information in your back-office systems, whether it's order status, inventory counts, billing, or vendor data. By marrying that information with your front-office sales, service, and marketing activities, your team is better equipped to deliver on its promises.

Tame dysfunctional processes

Tame business processes that are currently unstructured, unmonitored, unmanaged, unknown and unruly. Overstuffed with inefficiencies, manual tasks, and disjointed transitions from one process step to the next, these processes form in the seams and shadows of the enterprise, representing all the work involved in end-to-end processes that packaged apps cannot address[3].

Provide better tools for workers

Help workers who need to use multiple systems to get their work done, often with a combination of processes, data sources, and spreadsheets. Alleviate the need for workers to have to work around predefined processes in some way, especially for collaboration and communication. Reduce the numerous transfers of tasks required between people and systems that often cause breakdowns and inefficiencies, and decrease the time required for these transfers.

---

[3] The Forrester Wave: Dynamic Case Management, Q1 2011

Finding a solution

As the Big Shift takes hold, companies are no longer places that exist to drive down costs by getting increasingly bigger. They're places that support and organize talented individuals to get better faster by working with others. The rationale of the firm shifts from scalable efficiencies to scalable learning – the ability to improve performance more rapidly and learn faster by effectively integrating more and more participants distributed across traditional institutional boundaries.
– John Hagel III, John Seely Brown, Lang Davison, *The Power of Pull: How Small Moves, Smartly Made, Can Set Big Things in Motion*

The remainder of this book is devoted to exploring how to achieve these objectives by establishing one-to-one relationships with every single one of your customers through technology – without them having to think in terms of IT projects.

It includes:

1. The challenges on the road to becoming a Customer Company
2. The proposed solution: Smart Process Applications (SPA)
3. Prerequisites for successful SPA implementation
4. The anatomy of a SPA Builder
5. The role of IT with SPA
6. Benefits of SPA
7. How to accelerate your adoption of Force.com with SPA
8. Conclusion

There are also 2 Appendices:
1. Introducing a Force.com-based SPA Builder
2. SPA case studies

Challenges on the road to becoming a Customer Company

Value creation is more and more based on intellectual activity rather than manual dexterity or brute strength. But we continue to use the management and organizational structures that worked for the factory and the field. Here success was determined by standardization and efficiency. These in turn demanded adherence to a set procedure. We used people as cogs in a machine when we could not devise a machine to do the job.
– Ian James, The Process Consultant

For the past two decades, much of the focus for information technology deployment has been on automating or even eliminating less-skilled jobs. This has been largely effective, and organizations today are able to do far more with fewer people. Workers today spend less of their time on routine tasks than was possible just ten years ago.

A knowledge worker is someone who knows more about his or her job than anyone else in the organization.

- Peter Drucker

These types of automated systems are givens, commodities that can add little additional value to the organization. What are left are the unstructured business processes that have received little attention from management until now.

Harnessing and coordinating these unstructured processes in a way that provides customers with a consistent, cohesive and agile experience is what is needed to become a Customer Company.

How do these unstructured processes manifest themselves in the organization?

Wilson, what is a knowledge worker, and do we have any on staff?

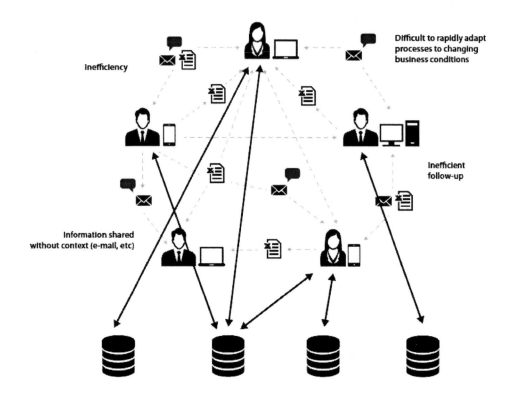

Figure 3: If your company looks anything like this, becoming a Customer Company is going to be a bit of a challenge. But it can be done!

On the frontlines with Fred

All employees are ultimately knowledge workers and the role of the firm is to both encourage and support problem solving by all employees.
- John Hagel III, John Seely Brown and Lang Davison, *Harvard Business Review Blog Network*

The frontlines of the organization, where the company interacts with its customers, is a dynamic and unpredicatable world where workers must respond quickly to constant change and deal with an environment full of exceptions.

This requires workers to interact with disparate systems, rationalize multiple versions of data, deal with fragmented business processes, and constantly communicate and collaborate with others.

Greatest Productivity Hurdles Knowledge Workers Face in a Typical Workday

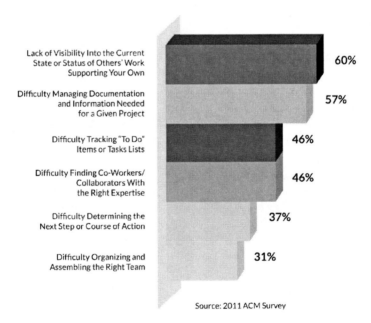

Lack of Visibility Into the Current State or Status of Others' Work Supporting Your Own	60%
Difficulty Managing Documentation and Information Needed for a Given Project	57%
Difficulty Tracking "To Do" Items or Tasks Lists	46%
Difficulty Finding Co-Workers/ Collaborators With the Right Expertise	46%
Difficulty Determining the Next Step or Course of Action	37%
Difficulty Organizing and Assembling the Right Team	31%

Source: 2011 ACM Survey

In this environment, there is not a lot of time to think about being a Customer Company.

Fred is one of these workers. Let's explore his world.

Figure 4: *Fred is a typical knowledge worker. His work requires improvisation and the use of judgment in ambiguous situations. Many of these improvisations require interactions with his fellow humans. In this sense, all employees are ultimately knowledge workers and the role of the firm is to both encourage and support problem solving by all employees.*

Fred has a lot of problems to deal with

Fred lives in a dynamic and unpredictable world. His success lies in his ability to coordinate many information feeds, harness personal connections, and process interactions. His ability to navigate this maze effectively and quickly is based on knowledge that is rarely written down or readily available to others.

His actions and decisions are often driven by unexpected events and exceptions to documented business processes. He has to deal with the growing amount of information and the growing complexity of relationships and regulations in the global economy.

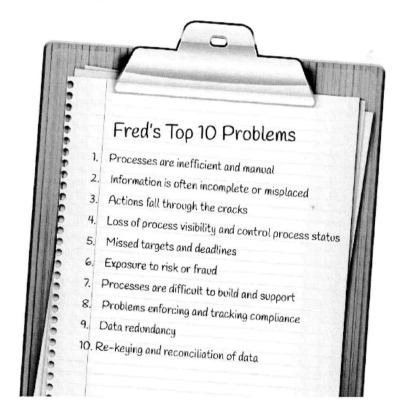

Fred's Top 10 Problems

1. Processes are inefficient and manual
2. Information is often incomplete or misplaced
3. Actions fall through the cracks
4. Loss of process visibility and control process status
5. Missed targets and deadlines
6. Exposure to risk or fraud
7. Processes are difficult to build and support
8. Problems enforcing and tracking compliance
9. Data redundancy
10. Re-keying and reconciliation of data

Let's look at some of the problems Fred must deal with in more detail.

Silos

Most of our companies are structured to solve 20th century problems. The customer idea is lost somewhere in the middle.
-Ranjay Gulati, Professor of Business Administration, Harvard Business School

The evil silo

Silos are often heavily guarded fortresses called the Marketing Department or Finance or Operations, which are protected by impenetrable vines of bureaucracy, entrenched interests and Established Ways of Doing Things.

Meet "the silos"

Silos limit the workers' access to knowledge about their customers and their opportunities to use that knowledge to better serve the marketplace.

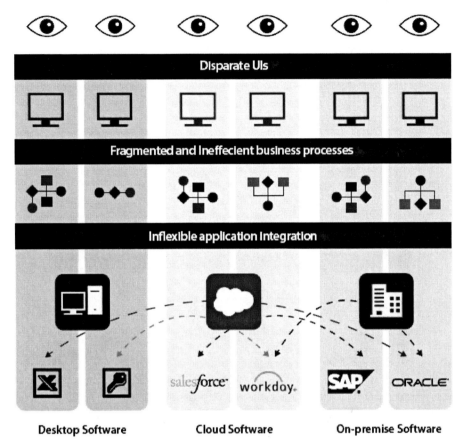

Figure 5: Silos obscure the overall visibility of work being done in the organization as a result of multiple interfaces, disjointed processes, and complex data integration.

There are many types of silos:

Collaborative and Communication silos

It is often very difficult for workers to collaborate effectively with users of other systems at the real-time point of decision. Emails and phone calls are poor mediums when the need to take action is now. Interaction between multiple departments that need to make a decision handled through email and telephone means no tracking and no automated ability to follow-up if tasks are slipping. As a result, business action is less than optimal, and valuable insights are lost.

For example, let's say you email a group of people using system A to assign them a task in system B to review a document shared in system C. The differences in access control and information architectures of A, B and C will inevitably lead to "I can't see the document" and "I can't log in to B" types of problems. And how do you reply? By email in A? As a comment in B or C? And given that it could be any of these, how do you search for a comment that you previously read and need to find again?

Figure 6: The lack of a common understanding of what needs to be done and the context in which it needs to be accomplished leads to less than optimum results.

Process silos

Front-, middle- and back-office functions are usually componentized and departmentalized. There is often limited and sometimes almost hostile interaction between the various parts of an organization's value chain, which discourages collaborative work and makes virtual teaming next to impossible.

Data silos

Data is typically organized into different systems that cannot talk to each other, resulting in the same data having to be keyed in multiple times. Where integration is attempted, there is the added complexity of each system having its own unique method of integration. Data silos force users to go to multiple applications and use multiple data sources to get a single task done.

Many users find themselves in the situation where they need to integrate data from a variety of applications to get their work done, and the only way to do it is to copy and paste it into a spreadsheet.

"No, it's MY data!"

In addition, data is often incomplete, missing, duplicated, or inaccurate. This makes many business processes inefficient, ineffective, and costly, increasing organizational risk. Employees will waste time looking for the data they need – or spend too little time and make decisions based on incomplete information.

Application silos

Billions of dollars are lost every year because information systems don't work together. A vast amount of unnecessary time is spent in every office in every corner of the world just trying to act as the glue between systems. This is particularly true when a single task that needs to be done requires information from more than one system. This means that a user has to take the time to compose the information they need to complete the task. Not only does it waste time, it is prone to error and can impair decision making.

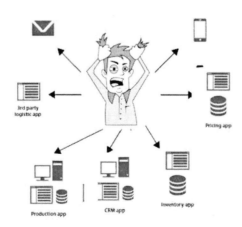

Work transitions

Teamwork fails most often in the moments between us.
- Ian James, The Process Consultant

Because of the variable nature of front-office work, the relay of information from worker to worker – much like the passing of the baton in a relay race – is fraught with potential problems. These problems include unnecessary time wasted between transitions, hand-off failures, miscommunication, and the lack of critical information needed to deal with expectations and to make the right decision.

The failure of work transitions is like the invisible killer disease pervading the organization. It spreads through email, status meetings, phone calls. Everyone is good at getting their own tasks done, then they hand the project off like a baton in a relay race, and it's "no longer their problem," so the project lays there, waiting for the next person to pick it up.

"What good is technology if it takes six seconds to send a message but six months to get someone to act on it?!"

The issue with this is that until someone else picks it up, it's no one's problem, and it can end up sitting, unfinished, for long periods of time. People like to think that once they hand it off, someone else will immediately pick it up, but this is not always the case.

A good example of the problems inherent in the relay of work is the approvals process, a critical component of a smooth and efficient business. Approval processes can be long and drawn out, and management may forget to respond to employees' email requests. Once an employee sends out the request, they may move on to the next task until they get a reply. If that reply never comes, the task doesn't get completed.

Emails can be missed, information might be missing, or people might simply forget about their task and let the baton drop. For example, you might know that a purchase order needs to be reviewed by three different colleagues, but you simply forgot to put the third name in the "to" line of the email that you are manually sending out. Small, manual mistakes like that impact how fast your processes get completed and, in the worst case, they can lead to conflicts and bigger problems down the line.

When the baton is finally picked up, it is often missing some key ingredients for that person to be successful during the next stage of the process. For instance, they may see that an unusual decision has been made. Instead of being updated with the reasoning for it, they may spend their time trying to find answers and get approvals before moving on.

Transitioning work in a virtual world

The increasing dispersion of the workforce across time and space makes the smooth transition of work from one employee to another increasingly difficult to manage and control, and increases the potential time between events actually occurring and the relevant people/systems being aware of them so they can take the necessary action.

This is only further exacerbated by the need of organizations to include freelance work and outsourced work. Transitioning work is hard enough within an organization, let alone throughout different organizations with different standards and practices.

Lag time

Most types of software – in particular, personal productivity applications, ERP, and CRM solutions – focus on reducing task time. Task time is the time process participants actually spend working on the tasks. While this is important to improve quality and simplify task execution, it is often not enough to truly improve overall process efficiency. Even if task time is reduced by 50%, the overall impact on the process time may only be 10%.

To get significant productivity gains, the focus must be not only on task time, but on reducing the lag time as processes flow across the organization. "Lag time" refers to the amount of time wasted when tasks are in transit or waiting in the in-baskets of the person responsible for getting them done. The dead time adds nothing of value to the business.

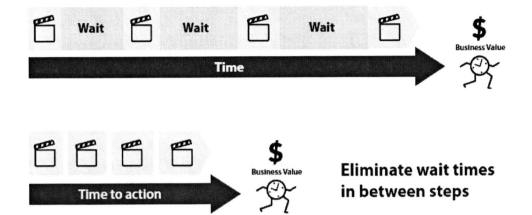

Figure 7: The typical nature of a complete business process today is a point of action followed by a delay, and a subsequent point of action followed by another delay, with this cycle repeated until the full process is finally executed. These rampant spans of inaction manifest themselves in market delays and operational delays.

Cycle time

The speed at which a process can be completed can be impacted by[4]:

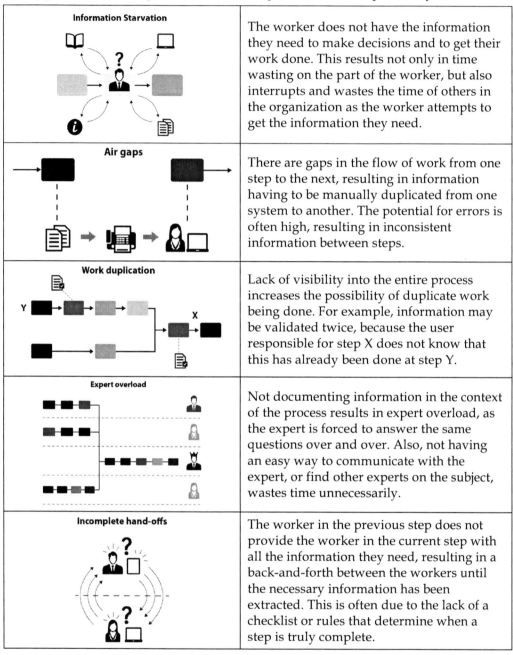

Information Starvation	The worker does not have the information they need to make decisions and to get their work done. This results not only in time wasting on the part of the worker, but also interrupts and wastes the time of others in the organization as the worker attempts to get the information they need.
Air gaps	There are gaps in the flow of work from one step to the next, resulting in information having to be manually duplicated from one system to another. The potential for errors is often high, resulting in inconsistent information between steps.
Work duplication	Lack of visibility into the entire process increases the possibility of duplicate work being done. For example, information may be validated twice, because the user responsible for step X does not know that this has already been done at step Y.
Expert overload	Not documenting information in the context of the process results in expert overload, as the expert is forced to answer the same questions over and over. Also, not having an easy way to communicate with the expert, or find other experts on the subject, wastes time unnecessarily.
Incomplete hand-offs	The worker in the previous step does not provide the worker in the current step with all the information they need, resulting in a back-and-forth between the workers until the necessary information has been extracted. This is often due to the lack of a checklist or rules that determine when a step is truly complete.

---

[4] Adapted from Ian James, The Process Consultant

Exception handling

For the average knowledge worker, exceptions are the rule. If the process went the same way each time, there would be no need for their specialized knowledge and decision-making skills. But that doesn't mean that we've figured out a way to handle exceptions smoothly and efficiently. Knowledge workers end up asking the same questions over and over again.

For example, a significant amount of time is wasted trying to identify the correct people required to help find an answer or determine whether an unusual request should be approved. In those situations, workers lack a single source of trusted answers to common questions and have difficulty finding the appropriate people to get involved in developing an answer. Similar problems occur repeatedly because the interactions with the customer and relevant functions are never formally documented in a context that makes them easy to find.

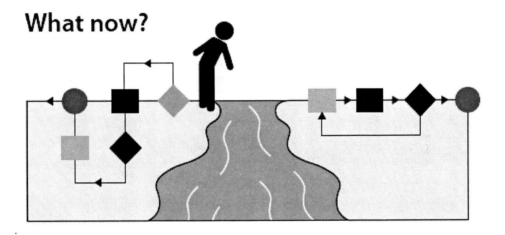

The more rigid the process, the more difficult it is to deal with exceptions. People need to find an alternative way to manage that particular instance of the process. So they turn to email and continue until they can get it back into the standard workflow. Email becomes the default workflow tool.

Dysfunctional business processes

The problem is that at a lot of big companies, process becomes a substitute for thinking. You're encouraged to behave like a little cog in a complex machine.

- Elon Musk, co-founder of Tesla Motors and PayPal

Processes involving knowledge workers are fluid and adaptable. The people involved interact in a world of fuzzy decisions, work in the gray area of abstract concepts, and tend to be highly unpredictable, often changing things and tinkering with the process rules.

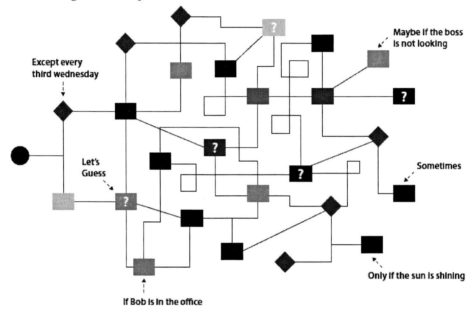

Figure 8: A typical dysfunctional business process[5]

This leads to a wide array of dysfunctional processes:

Disjointed process

Each department has its own business process, which doesn't integrate with those of other departments.

Untamed process

A haphazard approach results in processes that lack structure and, over time, become laden and bloated with non-value-added activity. Weak "solutions" are slapped on like Band-Aids – which only makes the untamed processes more inefficient.

Dumb processes

Dumb processes are processes without rules, analytics or a learning capability; or with rules that constrain participants from improving or forcing a customer down a path they don't want to go.

Dark processes

Dark processes take place in the shadows with no visibility to management.

Implied processes

Processes are implied in a flat, monolithic, static, inert application, making them difficult to understand and improve.

Fragile processes

When a process is used to make an organization's work uniform and done in exactly the same way, then the workers in that organization lose the ability to respond to unanticipated events. The organization becomes fragile and liable to break when external pressures change.

Rigid processes

Rigid processes surface where statements like "we can't do it that way" and "it would be too hard to change our process to allow for that" are commonplace.

DILBERT © 1994 Scott Adams. Used By permission of UNIVERSAL UCLICK. All rights reserved.

Cemented processes

Static processes automated by traditional BPM are often hard to change, and therefore remain static, causing opportunities to go to waste. In addition, organizations have customized applications where processes are implemented through hard coding.

Complex processes

> *Complexity has become the silent killer of profitable growth in business.*
> -   Chris Zook, *Desperately Seeking Simplicity*, Harvard Business Review

Often, antiquated enterprise systems impose complicated processes on employees. BPM systems have morphed from simple process automation and management into a much broader, infrastructure-type commitment that is often too complex, requiring significant IT resources and long lead times.

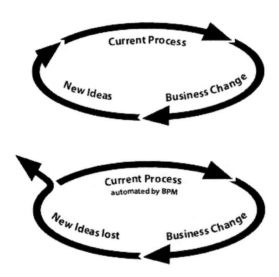

Figure 9: New ideas don't get implemented because of the time and cost to make them, especially when windows of opportunity close increasingly quickly.

The extended organization

The winning 21st century social enterprise will focus on selecting and managing expert suppliers and perform less rowing and more steering.
– Cognizant, *Build a Modern Social Enterprise to Win in the 21st Century*

A business is no longer an independent structure of supply and demand. It is more like an ecosystem that includes virtually anyone who wants to contribute to or benefit from the base offerings of the cornerstone company.

Figure 10: Its getting hard to define what a "company" is these days. The boundary between the enterprise and its vendors, partners and even competitors is becoming more and more blurred.

For example, if you own a Toshiba laptop computer that is under warranty and it breaks and you call Toshiba to have it repaired, Toshiba will tell you to drop it off at a UPS store and have it shipped it to Toshiba, and it will get repaired and then be shipped back to you. But UPS doesn't just pick up and deliver your Toshiba laptop. UPS actually repairs the computer in its own UPS-run workshop dedicated to computer repairs. So who does the guy in brown at your door work for? Toshiba? UPS? Or some third organization?

Boundaries between organizations are becoming more and more blurred as tasks and complete processes are outsourced to other companies across the globe. How do you facilitate an extended organization to support efficient outsourcing, manage globalization and implement virtual business networks?

Inter-organizational Business Processes

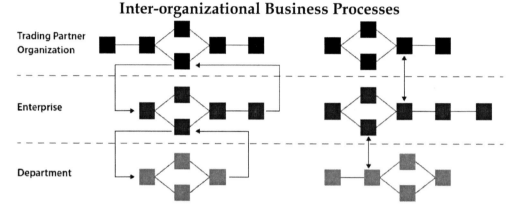

Figure 11: Companies recognize that they must become more adept at managing external as well as internal operations, so there is an escalating demand for better inter-enterprise collaboration, coordination, and communication.

Outsourcing

> *Until now, it made sense to contain resources and processes within the enterprise because it incurred too much friction and cost to go outside for them. Today, the opposite is true. It takes too much time and expense to acquire or build stuff in-house if it's already available on-demand from the cloud. The most successful, efficient organizations are those that can easily connect to and harness those cloud resources.*
> - Phil Wainewright, *From fixed to frictionless enterprise*

Customer Companies need to think more creatively about who performs which elements of the value and supply chains and where this work gets done.

For example, rather than owning and managing their own transportation fleets, some organizations are now using service providers to perform third-party logistics. Similarly, businesses are breaking apart their finance function and moving elements like expense processing to providers with expertise in that area.

This requires tight but flexible integration between companies with transparent processes and info flowing freely between the partners. But the outsourcing of process steps is not possible if the process is "locked" inside enterprise systems. Being able to quickly build applications that can facilitate the outsourcing of various steps in a business process is critical to the success of the virtual organization.

Outsourcing obviously increases the risk of coordination and integration, such as managing service level agreements and handoffs. Trying to create enterprise-wide business processes across different business units and systems was hard enough when everything was *inside* an organization. When businesses start to move data and systems to the cloud, they very quickly end up doubling process challenges.

The black hole of external processes

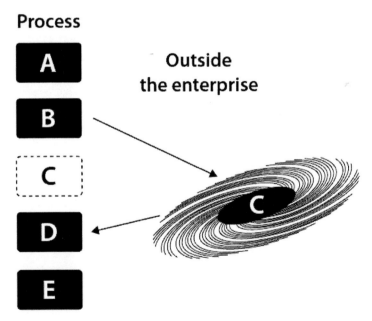

Figure 12: The rise in outsourcing and freelancing has led to a rise in external silos, which exist outside the organization and have no connection to the organization's resources. These processes may as well occur in a black hole, for all your organization knows about them.

An example of this is health care delivery, where elements of the process (e.g., reading x-rays) are handed off to external contractors who must have access to certain data, and return other data upon completion of their discrete task.

Companies can more easily harvest the talents of people working outside corporate boundaries if they can rapidly create highly customized applications that cater to the specific needs of each relationship.

This makes it more feasible to involve customers, suppliers, small specialist businesses, and independent contractors in the creation of products and services.

Virtual teams

> *The virtualization of work: the disaggregation of end-to-end value chains performed by a single company, into a networked collaboration, in which each company contributes its core specialization.*
> -Geoffrey Moore, *The Future of Work: A New Approach to Productivity and Competitive Advantage*

Next-generation enterprises will need to enable virtual teams to collaborate across geographies, time zones and functions. Virtual teams need a cohesive, automated and reliable way to share schedules, documents and artifacts; identify who has the information they're seeking; keep each other up to date; conduct meetings; post updates; disseminate critical information on a timely basis; and more. They need the flexibility to choose and source value chain elements from anywhere, disaggregating people from functions.

Looser organizational structures require technologies that support virtual teams of specialists scattered around the globe who can collaborate independent of location, time zone, technology, or language. These technologies must also support the instant reconfiguration of such teams. Teams that are formed quickly must be able to define their work environment and address many of their own needs as they arise.

Globalization

Globalization often requires engaging a local partner who understands a company's marketplace and can reduce misunderstandings. It is usually faster, less costly, and less risky to partner with a local company in a new and unfamiliar market. It is impractical to set up an IT support structure in these new markets, including the need to adjust for local rules and regulations, currency and language. Your organization cannot be trapped by the limitations of your information systems. To avoid chaos, there must be some structure and control to keep all the members of the global enterprise flying in formation.

Large, globally deployed systems can also encounter challenges addressing specific or local needs that are not widely shared in the industry or worldwide. For example, locally relevant information missing from the company workflow may result in holes that people have to fill with other locally created or purchased systems, or with homemade spreadsheets.

Business networks

The development of highly collaborative, high-complexity challenges require investing in relationship management. From the making of a movie to the development of a next-generation airliner, or the commercialization of a novel therapy, the focus is on leveraging a wide range of technologies and expertise to tackle a novel set of challenges, collaboratively creating not only new products or services but also whole new systems and categories that simply did not exist before.
-Philip Lay and Geoffrey Moore, *Business Network Transformation: IT's Next Great Opportunity to Shine*

Increasingly often, projects require a significant amount of capital, or a wide variety of talent, that cannot be accomplished by the efforts of any single enterprise. New market opportunities are being unlocked by combining the products and services of the business network participants in creative ways and leveraging each other's market access and infrastructure on a global basis.

This raises the need for business networks, defined as groups of companies that work together toward a specific objective for mutual benefit. The unique thing about business networks is that they can come together to work on a specific project, and then dissolve as they move their focus to other tasks that require a different set of skills.

The pace at which these business networks can be created and transformed is likely to increase rapidly. This will lead to more symbiotic relationships between organizations, with the need to provide ad hoc collaborative and other information technology services.

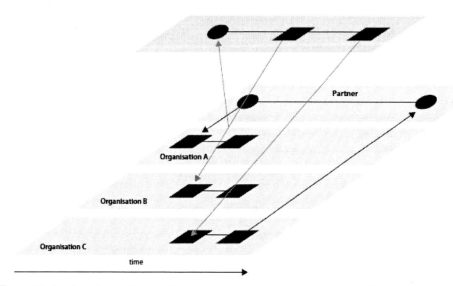

Figure 13: In effect, the need to operate as a collaborative business network is built into the very structure of the problems these companies must address.

Sidebar: The danger of BYOA

There has been a lot of focus on BYOD – "bring your own device" – as a problem that corporate IT needs to deal with.

But the impact of BYOD is nothing compared to the coming-to-you-soon impact of BYOA – "bring your own application."

BYOA is probably where BYOD was about three years ago. Now would be the time for IT to get ahead of it.

BYOA starts with consumer-focused applications with freemium models that enable employees to start using them without any company expenditure. Given the lack of real alternatives, it's not surprising that knowledge workers have embraced these sleek, free productivity tools over creaking old enterprise systems – or ancient tools like MS Access and Lotus Notes.

Most of these services store data on the provider's servers, which has obvious implications for the company's data security, discoverability and accountability. BYOA can also lead to the fragmentation of the company's collective knowledge across a wide range of disparate services. It is more likely than not that different departments will pick different, competing tools, and employees in another region pick yet another tool, perhaps one in a different language. The result is that data, information, and discussions are scattered across a range of incompatible services.

Welcome to the new cloud-based Shadow IT 2.0. Just like before – but much worse – the result will be a complete mishmash of solutions strewn all over the enterprise, with little control and even less visibility.

BYOA is going to have a major impact on an organization's ability to become a Customer Company. This is something every organization needs to think about.

Sidebar: Filling a Big Business Gap

In their seminal paper *Smart Process Applications Fill a Big Business Gap*, Forrester provides two good examples of companies experiencing the kind of challenges above[6]:

- A healthcare executive struggled with supply chain processes. An executive in a large hospital chain found his organization struggling to get essential work done. The business unit invested in an older application built on a straight-through-processing BPM tool that wasn't robust enough for the complexities of its buying process, nor could the application handle all the different options required for internal and external collaboration. People ended up working around the solution that was supposed to help them. Working outside the application is an example of an untamed process that needed a smart process app — only it didn't yet exist. As a result, he says, "We had very, very deep struggles to get the work done."

- A two-year-old startup couldn't find packaged software to support decentralized operations. Although this organization started small, it was growing quickly into a complex business, with decentralized sales partners working collaboratively to engage with customers and to negotiate complex contracts. In addition, it had a community of customers and business partners requiring customer care, warehousing, and logistics services based on task-oriented collaboration. The company considered buying packaged solutions for warehousing, accounting, and CRM but determined that these solutions could not handle its requirements for internal and external collaboration, mobility, incoming documents, content creation, frequent changes, and monitoring social sentiment. The startup was concerned with dealing with growth and rising complexity; growing, without creating bureaucracy; avoiding software development; staying focused on customer engagement; and managing a business with independent workers. It found that traditional software would not fit the bill.

---

[6] **Forrester,** *Smart Process Applications Fill a Big Business Gap, August 8, 2012*

Introducing Smart Process Applications (SPA)

If I had asked people what they wanted, they would have said faster horses.
-Henry Ford

In this period of profound change, many of the current orthodoxies about business opportunity, business models and the technology tools used to run enterprises are under significant stress.
- Cognizant Center for the Future of Work

In any deep transformation, industries do not so much adopt the new body of technology as encounter it, and as they do so they create new ways to profit from its possibilities.
–W. Brian Arthur, *The Second Economy*

Many of the challenges explored in the previous chapter cannot be addressed effectively by the tools we use today – custom applications, business process management (BPM) suites, or the default method of Excel + email.

Recognizing the need for a new approach, the analyst firm Forrester has defined a new category of software called Smart Process Applications (SPA)[7].

SPA is focused on supporting business activities that are:

1. People-intensive
2. Highly variable
3. Loosely structured
4. Subject to frequent change

---

[7] Forrester, *Smart process applications fill a big business gap*

Where Smart Process Applications fit in your organization

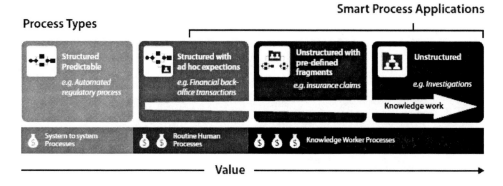

Source: Adapted from Sandy Kemsley

Figure 14: Every organization has many processes that are similar in name between businesses, but are actually often highly customized. This customization is often handled in an unstructured or semi-structured manner.

Being a new category of software, the Forrester definition is sufficiently vague enough that it can be (and has been) interpreted in many different ways. Some organizations look at SPA as nothing more than an extension of BPM, or perhaps subsumed under the ACM and DCM monikers. There is, of course, a great deal of overlap among these terms, and there are many debates around the Internet trying to figure out which is "better."

> SPA amplifies human capability through a mixture of process, automation, and collaboration.

But it's appropriate that there is a new name for a solution that focuses *solely* on the problem of human-powered "smart" business processes, where **the objective is to introduce a measure of structure and control into the everyday interactions between humans to assist them in reaching a common, predefined goal.**

Since the opportunities to use technology to automate processes through the elimination of manual work are dwindling, what remains are those processes that are human-intensive. This is where the action is, where organizations can really make a difference.

These human-based processes or activities range from relatively simple cases involving one to three people in handling and resolving a case, to service delivery situations involving similar numbers of people handling less-predictable and less-structured service problems, to some or many people working on a project over time, to many people working on a complex operation in unstructured conditions. The goal of smart process applications is to improve this range of human-based activities or processes[8].

Unlike structured processes, where applications can replace people, software can enhance the capabilities of the people doing unstructured work. And because this work commonly provides the most value in modern organizations, improving unstructured business processes can generate the most competitive advantage today. Smart process applications go a long way toward facilitating the needs of organizations in their quest to become a "smart" Customer Company.

> SPA brings order, tracking and management to unstructured, interdependent and extended processes that are currently executed primarily via email, spreadsheets and meetings.

SPA supports the way people actually do work, how they use their problem-solving skills and how they make decisions that drive a process forward.

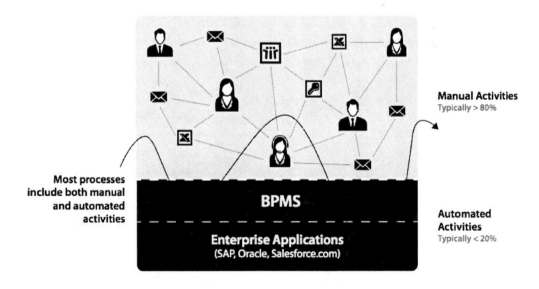

Manual Activities
Typically > 80%

Most processes include both manual and automated activities

BPMS

Enterprise Applications
(SAP, Oracle, Salesforce.com)

Automated Activities
Typically < 20%

---

[8] Ian James, The Process Consultant

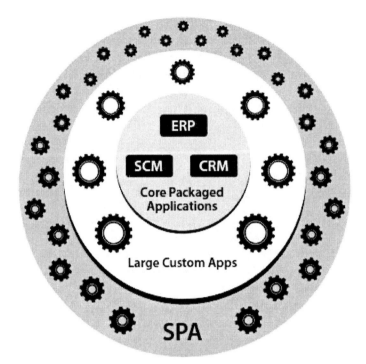

Figure 15: Solid core, flexible boundary. SPA is found at the edge of the organization, where the opportunity for innovation, value-creation and external interaction takes place.

SPA defined

> *The cognitive model is to treat the computer not as a box, but a door.*
> *It's something you need to get through to get to the value on the other*
> *side. People don't want a door with 32 different kinds of handles.*
> –Clay Shirky, *Here Comes Everybody: The Power of Organizing Without*
> *Organizations*

Smart

Forrester refers to the "smart" in SPA to mean, "charged by advancing analytics." The analytics provide the intelligence needed to interpret signals that indicate where things are headed and the capability to proactively move in that direction.

But the "smart" in SPA also includes the "smarts" that knowledge workers need to get their work done. Any tool that is to meet the needs of the knowledge worker requires the ability for them to apply their knowledge throughout the execution of the solution they build.

Process

SPA addresses the fact that traditional business process management (BPM) is ill suited to the needs of the knowledge worker. The focus of SPA is on people, not systems; collaboration, not automation.

Applications

The applications in SPA are not the traditional large, inert, static, monolithic, developer-centric applications that solve a general problem. SPA recognizes that with the advent of mobile, the very nature of applications is changing. These applications are small, dynamic, user-driven slices of single-purpose functionality highly customized to the needs of users at the time – and location – they need it.

Let's look at each of these in turn.

Smart

> *The health, competitive power, and even survival of an enterprise*
> *largely depends on its ability to understand and harness the power of*
> *knowledge workers who are enabled to take responsibility for*
> *providing automatic solutions to meet many of their business needs.*
> –   IBM System Journal, *SOA meets situational applications: Examples and lessons*
> *learned*

The advanced analytics aspect of "smart" in SPA is addressed later. This chapter focuses on the "smarts" of knowledge workers.

Knowledge workers need to build their own solutions

Fred the knowledge worker is required to make decisions and judgments based on his knowledge.

Fred must decide what methods and steps to use in order to achieve a given outcome, usually by processing information and doing something with it. In some cases the decision making can be automated, but the unpredictability of the work performed by knowledge workers makes automation difficult.

Building traditional developer-driven solutions simply don't work for Fred, because:

"One- size-fits-all" is not appropriate for knowledge workers. Knowledge workers have individual learning and communication styles; they need the ability to approach their activities in the way they feel most comfortable.

Knowledge workers need to respond quickly to constant change. The world of the knowledge worker is always in flux. Therefore, in order to adapt effectively, they need to be able to do things like modify rules without waiting for the IT department.

The world of the knowledge worker is not easily accessible to outsiders. Most of their knowledge is inside their heads – they just "know" how to do the things they need to do and find it difficult to explain to those on the outside.

Knowledge workers don't like to be told what to do. No one knows better than you do how to get your work done, so why should someone else be telling you how to do it? Knowledge workers are like artists. They want (and usually need) creativity and variation in their work, and often resent attempts to "streamline" or automate their work in any way—especially when imposed from the outside.

The world of the knowledge worker is full of exceptions. In the world of the knowledge worker, things are messy. People like to tinker, to change things. People are unpredictable. Exceptions are a way of life and too numerous to be planned for in advance. This is a world very much disconnected from the world of transaction-based systems.

Users need to build their own solutions. There is no longer any time to waste for IT to build solutions. The only way to address the day-to-day needs of customers is to give workers better tools so they can produce their own solutions, with as little involvement from IT as possible.

ONLY AN EMPOWERED
EMPLOYEE CAN SERVE
THE NEEDS OF AN
EMPOWERED CUSTOMER.

Figure 16: "In the future of work, employees must be empowered to operate at their full potential, and this requires a workplace that has freed itself of unnecessary and debilitating boundaries. It is only then that companies can hope to meet the business challenges of the fast-changing global economy." –Cognizant, Future of work enabler: Worker Empowerment

The paucity of tools for knowledge workers

For decades, many IT organizations have been dealing with developers outside of the IT department as if they were insurgents – their weapons were Excel and Access.
–Mike Rollings (Gartner), *Citizen Development: Reinventing the Shadows of IT*

Knowledge workers need to use multiple systems to get their work done, often with a combination of enterprise process applications, other data sources, and end-user computing tools such as spreadsheets. They frequently have to work around the predefined process in some way, especially for collaboration and customer communication. The systems may be augmented or integrated in an ad hoc, unsupported manner in an attempt to improve the functionality and information context.

Few organizations, until now, have actively supported the efforts of their knowledge workers to solve problems themselves.

But this doesn't mean that knowledge workers have simply accepted this. They have gone off and found whatever tools they could to help them get their jobs done.

The tools knowledge workers use today to help them achieve their objectives are like the land of mutant toys.

They do just a fraction of the job needed, they can't work together, and they create a slew of problems, including:

- Isolation
- Duplication of data
- Lack of security
- Lack of scalability
- Lack of oversight
- Need for hardware and software
- Inability to be included in workflows
- Inability to leverage new technology

Indiscriminate use and abuse of spreadsheets is typically rampant, resulting in:

- spreadsheets being emailed around the organization for data collection and synthesis;
- spreadsheets being used as part of a core process without anyone really knowing how they work;

- spreadsheets so massive that a human can't possibly comprehend them;
- employees spending an inordinate amount of time cutting and pasting, updating, consolidating and re-entering data onto spreadsheets;
- frequent instances of out-of-date information in spreadsheets;
- multiple versions of the same spreadsheet circulating around the company; and
- spreadsheets being used to produce recurring, error-prone reports.

Errors in Spreadsheets
Errors are more frequent than most assume

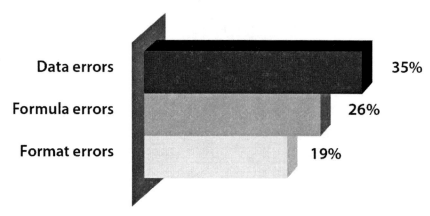

Data errors   35%

Formula errors   26%

Format errors   19%

Source: Ventana Research Spreadsheets in
Today's Enterprise Benchmark Research

Sidebar: Marc Benioff on "Productivity Applications"

You look at products like Lotus Notes and it's a product that was conceived before Mark Zuckerberg, the Founder of Facebook, was. The reality is that it's not a humorous joke. It was a great product at the time, but IBM has done a terrible job in terms of keeping it fresh.

Customers have been running this technology for two and three decades. They are hiring people out of school and they are coming into these "Productivity Applications" and are saying, "I don't know how to use this, this is not how I work. Where is my iPad? Where is my iPhone? Where is my BlackBerry? Where is my graphical user interfaces?" [Companies] are like, "well, this is graphical user interface" and "this is Windows." It's just junk and that's what Lotus Notes is honestly...

... Just look at the terrible job IBM has done with their software strategy. They've had to move to an acquisition strategy because they let these kinds of core franchises erode. They turned them into cash cows and now they are getting trampled by these next generation products.

It's still Sharepoint!

I think [Microsoft] SharePoint is very much the same thing. It's kind of the grandmother's attic. These customers throw everything into it and then they can't find it and they don't know what's up there, and they don't know how to get it out.[9]

---

[9] Marc Benioff, BusinessCloud9, November, 2010

Process

The BPM tools on the market today provide solutions to business people, but are not designed for business people to actually use to solve their problems. BPM is no help with unstructured processes. Nor is classic project management. That too, relies on the ability to plan an outcome. We need a different approach.
-Ian James, The Process Consultant

BPM provides solutions.

What's needed is a way for knowledge workers to build their own solutions.

Most organizations have spent years automating their business processes with BPM, which means they have already gotten most of the benefits available in this area. Unfortunately, a clear majority of the business processes in your company are probably unstructured, yet these are the hardest to automate with BPM software.

Rote work seldom creates value. Any task that can be reduced to a predictable set of steps can often be done by machine, delegated to less-skilled workers, or outsourced to a lower-cost region.

What is needed now is to tackle processes that can't easily be mapped, streamlined or automated. Any process that calls for knowledge and judgment is vital to creating competitive advantage. This is the space in which knowledge workers thrive and where real value can be achieved.

As succinctly described by Ian James[10]:

> These "unstructured" processes are less like an assembly line and are more like a pinball machine, where a transaction bounces from person to person in an unpredictable path with an uncertain outcome. Imagine how difficult it would be to predict and control the path of every ball that falls through a pinball machine. Yet this is what BPM software tries to do.

---

[10] This section on unstructured processes based on work by Ian James, The Process Consultant, at theprocessconsultant.com.

An unstructured process has many branches, calls for flexible routing, and generates variable results. An unstructured process depends on the knowledge, judgment and creativity of employees; that makes it difficult to automate. An unstructured process is seldom repeated, or else repeated with different paths and outcomes. A lot of information is required and generated along the way. For best results, employees must see the big picture and understand the roles, responsibilities, priorities, and deadlines of themselves and others.

These are the processes that truly add value and are worth investing in. Improving unstructured processes can yield tangible benefits such as lower costs, better quality, and higher employee satisfaction.

Why hire people for their judgment and creativity, train them extensively, and then constrain them in processes that leave no room for initiative? Unfortunately, this is precisely what BPM does when applied to an unstructured process.

BPM software was designed for yesterday's assembly lines, not today's knowledge-based economy. Most high-value business processes handled by office workers are not easy to map, streamline, or automate. Many creative knowledge workers instinctively resist any attempt to impose BPM software.

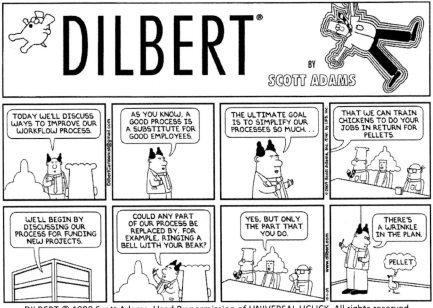

BPM versus SPA

*Businesses used to live or die on the quality of their tools: the business processes and solutions that they invested so heavily in. Today businesses live or die on their ability to adapt: their ability to **use the tools around them** to solve the problem (or capitalize on the opportunity) in front of them.*
- Peter Evans-Greenwood, *The New Instability: How globalization, cloud computing and social media enable you to create an unfair advantage*

BPM and SPA provide different starting points for looking at the world:

Ordered World	Complex World
Cause and effect can be precisely determined.	Cause and effect are intertwined and cannot be determined in advance.
Certain parties have control.	All parties have influence.
There is only one way ahead.	There are many possibilities for progress.
Large effects require enormous coordinated efforts.	Large effects come from small starts and positive feedback.
The future can be planned.	The future *emerges* from the combined actions of the players.
Top down.	Bottom up.
Complexity to simplicity.	Simplicity to complexity.

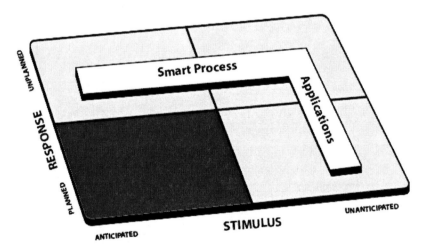

Figure 17: Unlike traditional BPM, SPA addresses unanticipated and unplanned events.

Whereas BPM is primarily focused on automation and integration, SPA is primarily focused on orchestration and coordination.

Here are some other differences:

BPM	SPA
BPM is a solution for getting repetitive work done as efficiently as possible.	SPA is a solution *builder*, a tool that helps users to get their work done as effectively as possible by making it easier for them to make the right decisions and take the right actions at the right time.
The measure of success is the increase of volume of throughput or work completed for an individual process.	The measure of success is the optimization of outcome for each individual instance of a process.
Tries to eliminate as much human involvement as possible through automation.	People are an inherent and desired part of the process.
Controls the process by defining it in advance.	Does not try to control the process, leaving it to the user to define as it happens.
Reduces the need for judgment. The process designer builds all the decisions about what happens into the process. People just need to follow along.	Gives the user control over what tasks get done and what sequence to follow.
The rigidity of process limits what users can do when there is a set of circumstances the process cannot deal with, leading to frustration of the "I-hate-this-stupid-system" variety.	Users have more, not less, control over their working day. They get to route things to the right people when they see the need, without any software barriers preventing them from doing so.
Typically considers only one process at a time.	Assumes people work in multiple processes at the same time.
Requires a trained resource to pre-program sequence and rules.	No training is required, and sequence and rules are added as needed.
Requires process diagrams that are difficult to create, keep up to date, and enforce. Even if they start off beautifully designed and highly effective, business processes naturally degrade over time, causing delays and errors.	Process diagrams are optional. A simple list of tasks is all that is needed to start a process. There is no need to attempt to map the un-mappable.

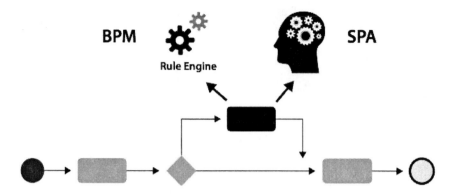

Figure 18: With BPM, the smarts of the process are provided primarily via a Rule Engine. With SPA, the smarts are provided primarily by the knowledge worker and analytics.

Applications

Mobility forces us to think of new ways to approach the market, customers and our channel. The technology really enables new ways of operating. It allows us to think in new ways about different business models and about how to approach the customer.
-Bill Blausey, Senior VP and CIO of Eaton Corporation

Mobile is the future delivery mechanism for applications. But mobile technology is forcing a major change in how applications are written and deployed.

Mobile applications need to confront these types of problems:

- Users can't navigate through a complex set of menus on a mobile device.

- Users can't easily "look up" information in legacy applications if there is something they need.

- Users can't easily use a screen that has lots of data and information on it that does not pertain to the task at hand.

- Users can't do swivel integration on a mobile device – apps need to bundle information in context from multiple legacy systems and from multiple sources.

As a result, mobile software solutions need to be small, highly targeted, single-function applications – like enter a request for parts, ship an order, or a check a flight schedule.

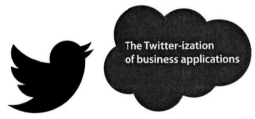

The Twitter-ization of business applications

Figure 19: Mobile forces the creation of short bursts of functionality in context.

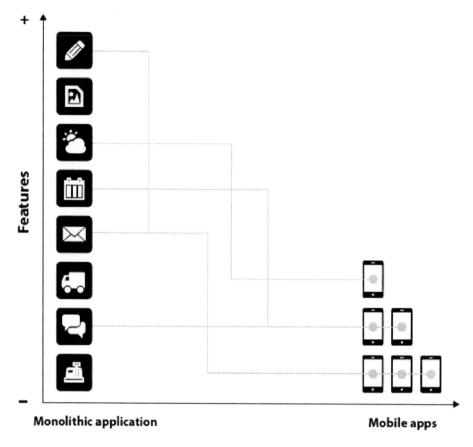

Figure 20: Mobile apps must include only a small number of specific elements of a traditional application to work effectively.

Instead of big-bang everything and everyone-at-once implementations, the need now is to create large numbers of small services (*micro moments*) that can be rapidly orchestrated into selected processes, and equally quickly changed again. This allows solutions to be small, experimental, innovative, and locally relevant.

These micro-apps also cannot take a "one-size-fits-all" approach; their evolution is inherently iterative, the lifecycle is dependent on succinct user requirements, and the focus is on the end user experience.

To be effective, mobile apps need to be very targeted and often single-function, such as checking flight arrivals, looking for contacts, tracking shipments, ordering spare parts, approving requests, or checking account balances. The objective is to provide simple features and functions with pre-populated data that make it as easy as possible for users to complete specific tasks.

Mobile apps are perfect for knowledge workers. Unlike factory workers, knowledge workers do not just do the same thing over and over again. Instead, knowledge workers are constantly trying to solve new problems. This constant need to innovate means that knowledge workers don't want big, static, end-to-end solutions. Instead, they need to use their knowledge, their smarts, to bring together snippets of functionality into the context of a particular challenge they are reacting to, or an opportunity they are pursuing.

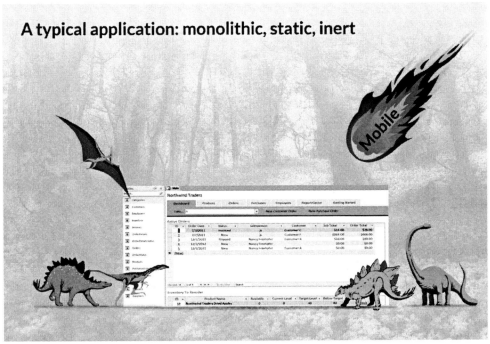

Figure 21: Mobile forces organizations to move away from brittle, monolithic, developer-centric applications solving a general problem, to agile, contextual, user-driven applications to support specific business objectives.

Traditional applications versus SPA

Many of the factors dictating how to build traditional applications in a traditional environment change with the development of situational applications on a digital business platform.

	Traditional Applications	SPA
Applications	A single, complex, multi-function, self-contained "package" of functionality with complex navigation schemes used by multiple business roles.	Multiple simple, intuitive, single-function apps synchronized with business roles. These apps can be orchestrated in a workflow as needed to accomplish business processes.
Development	Developers build large applications based on specifications given to them by users.	Users build small, process-driven applications with the help of developers as needed.
Growth	An application stays in the same form over a period of years.	SPA is considered a seed that will grow and evolve continuously.
Contributions	From time to time IT will incorporate new ideas into the application so it doesn't become out of touch with the real world.	SPA is enriched through the contributions of knowledgeable people, and important and relevant additions are constantly being incorporated.
Stakeholders	Line of Business executives, Corporate IT.	Individual users or self-organizing small teams.
Evolution	Top-down controlled, centrally driven, dependent on available funding.	Organic, based on user feedback and participation.
Time-to-value	Many months or years.	Days or weeks.
Development phases	Well defined, following agreed-to schedule (although with frequent schedule overruns).	No defined phases, milestones, or schedules – focusing on a good-enough solution to address an immediate need.
Functional requirements	IT needs to "freeze" requirements to move to development; change is discouraged.	Changes as business requirements change; encourages unintended uses.

	Traditional Applications	SPA
Funding	Often coincides with annual IT planning; requires approved budgets.	No formal budget; developed and run under the radar of corporate IT.
Stability	Fixed, highly stable.	Moving target and in a state of perpetual beta.
Governance	Centralized and formal.	Grassroots and community-based.
Adoption	Generalized.	Form-fit tools for very particular needs.
Ownership	Highly controlled environment.	Local team control; ownership mentality.
Cost	Cost is significant, so it is often shared by multiple sponsors.	Sponsors can spend far less and get exactly what they need.
Communication	Larger group means more chance of miscommunication.	Smaller group reduces time spent on communication; less chance of miscommunication.
Desired result	Focuses on doing the work in the correct manner.	Focuses on the desired result.
Motivation	Seeks to avoid failure. Concerned with maintaining the status quo.	Seeks success. Attempts to find new ways to perform tasks better.
Change	Reacts to change.	Anticipates change.

Example

In the example below, core business processes remain in place, but micro-apps have been created for mobile.

Note that there is an implied process here – the mobile apps are orchestrated as the traveler moves from reservation through travel to next reservation.

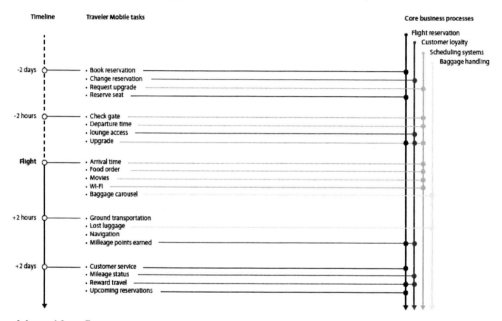

Customers micro-apps in the travel industry - without SPA

Adapted from Forrester

Figure 22: Every mobile app has to get its own information from one or more legacy applications.

This example becomes even more complex if work is being done by different organizations, each of which has its own systems. By definition, there is no centralized database, no integrated workflow, and no communication and collaboration medium.

So the only effective solution is to create a *virtual layer* on which all these entities can play.

Customers micro-apps in the travel industry - with SPA

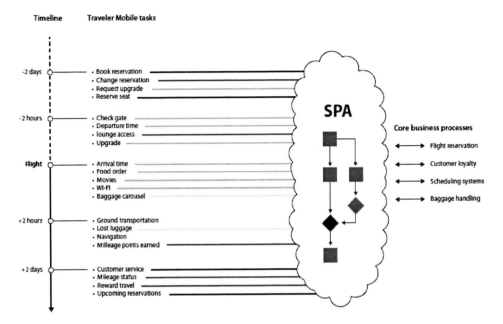

Adapted from Forrester

Figure 23: With SPA, it is much simpler to build and change mobile apps, since they don't have to be concerned about finding and integrating data from legacy systems on their own.

Bringing it all together

SPA needs to:
- *Manage applications in parallel as well as in series*
- *Manage people-intensive applications*
- *Decouple the process from the application*
- *Work both inside and outside the organization*
- *Be both continuous and discrete, and allow processes to change over time*
- *Put the process into the hands of the business user*

- Peter Fingar, *The Business Process Platform in the Sky*

Micro-apps must be orchestrated by insertion into complete business processes to meet their ultimate business objective. By doing this, users will see a micro-app appear in their activity feed when the system tells them they need to take action. It allows core systems to respond to process context, rather than driving processes around the limits of technology.

Instead of building applications and hard-coding business processes into the code, the new world of mobile requires the reverse approach – start with processes and build complete applications by orchestrating mobile-driven mini-apps.

Service technicians, for example, may need just six or seven apps that are crucial for performing their job on the road – like confirming an order is complete, or ordering a spare part for a repair. They don't need an entire "field technician application" involving complex navigation schemes and requiring hours of training. They just need highly purposeful, single-function micro-apps that are aligned with their role and intuitive to use, to ensure quick adoption. These micro-apps provide simple features and functions with pre-populated data to make it as easy as possible for users to complete specific tasks.

These "micro-apps" are then orchestrated to meet a particular business objective, like processing a service request. Therefore, there needs to be a way to create a flow that brings the micro-apps to life when needed.

By deconstructing processes, each step in the process can be executed by the best possible team or service, wherever they happen to be (including outside the organization). This provides much more flexibility and facilitates much better responsiveness.

In continuing with the service technician example, here is how small apps can make up a complete business process:

1. A technician does an inspection of a building. The technician starts up an inspection application. There is no need to type in or select the building, since the application already knows where the technician is.

2. The technician walks around the building, using their iPhone to answer questions regarding each aspect of the building – heating, loading dock, mold, etc. The technician takes a photo with the phone to record the element they are monitoring.

3. The system automatically triggers a notification to the appropriate vendor to take care of any problems found, sending along all the information recorded, including the relevant photo.

4. If replacement equipment is needed, a purchase order is created and a notification is sent to the purchasing department, and provisioned from the closest warehouse.

5. At the end of the inspection, a list of outstanding problems is sent to the support desk for follow-up.

6. Once the inspection is complete (e.g., all issues have been resolved), a notification is sent to the technician's manager for approval of the report. It's immediate, without any additional effort on the part of the technician or anyone else.

7. Any issues found along the way can be dealt with collaboratively. Special approvals or additional steps can be added into the process where needed.

Characteristics of SPA

Tools shape the solution. No one knew they needed a spreadsheet before Visicalc, or a home page before the World Wide Web.
–Jeff Tash, *Flashmap Systems*

Cloud brings chaos, and we need to start embracing it rather than just finding new ways to control it.
-Chris Wolf, Gartner vice president

The future lies in a world where business users appropriate tools to create solutions, and the value of a tool that everyone can use comes when everyone uses it for a thousand little things.

SPA makes processes targeted, dynamic and alive - users can "go with the flow" and easily adapt to changing circumstances.

To be successful, a management process tool has to strike a balance between giving the worker freedom to complete their work in a way that best suits their needs, while doing so in the context of the overall business objectives that work is designed to meet. The need for some element of structure and control provided by BPM remains, but with a lot more freedom and a lot less automation.

Rather than dictating the actions that people must take, SPA provides people with the tools and resources (including connections to other people) required for them to take initiative and creatively address opportunities as they arise.

Freedom in a framework

*A business-system structure consisting of **reusable** components **reconfigurable** in a **scalable** framework is the most effective model for creating adaptable systems.*
–Rick Dove, Paradigm Shift International

The way in which we currently build information systems favors equilibrium conditions because our tools and techniques do not handle transition states (the messiness of the real world, like melting ice) very well. But if change is constant, we have no choice but to understand and deal with it as best we can.

There is a middle ground between rigid processes and total chaos, and that is a framework that provides structure and control, but allows freedom when needed.

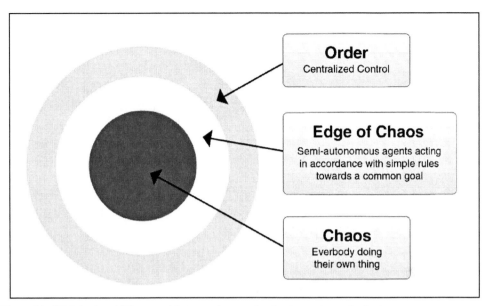

Figure 24: SPA is the middle ground between chaos and order to survive and adapt.

The flexible approach requires organizations to embrace uncertainty, dynamic demand, and some degree of chaos, and to learn to thrive on it.

The rest is left to the flexibility, adaptability, and creativity of the individual agents as the context continually changes.

The SPA framework provides consistency and structure, while allowing for local optimizations and agility that enable the organization to adapt and compete. Business units can take advantage of the flexibility of SPA to achieve their own local goals within a framework that drives a single organizational view.

A framework provides agility, lower risk, higher predictability and stability, and greater productivity.

Instead of dictating, the framework lets individual employees decide which activities are necessary and which pathways to follow to meet the requirements of their jobs. The balance between rigidity and chaos is created by providing ample information, empowering employees to make decisions, setting clear expectations, and spelling out what is acceptable to the company, with the ultimate goal being to inject an element of structure and control into business processes that don't have any.

Frameworks: Three types of construction toy systems

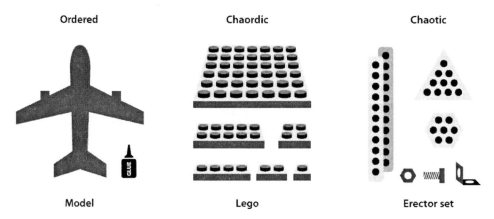

Ordered   Chaordic   Chaotic

Model   Lego   Erector set

Figure 25: Toy systems are a good metaphor, since the objective of construction toys is to facilitate the constant configuration and reconfiguration of objects. Legos straddle the fence between too much order, where nothing much happens in response to an environmental change, and too much chaos, where nothing much happens with coherency and purpose.

SPA works off a single platform

Unlike traditional applications or processes that are monolithic and self-contained, SPA solutions work off the same underlying platform. This is critical for SPA to work – there needs to be a common medium through which users, micro-apps and processes can communicate and interact.

By using a single platform, SPA shares the same data, social network, and user security. Any application has access to any data, flow or task. Therefore, workflows and business processes can be shared among customers, departments, and external agencies, all without disruption. With everyone using the same platform, there's no need to reproduce or copy-and-paste data into different systems depending on who is working from where.

The SPA framework protects users from themselves

Frameworks always need to negotiate a fine line between doing too much, which limits flexibility, and too little, which reduces effectiveness. Users are constrained so they don't make serious mistakes, and the framework is tolerant, making it easy to correct errors.

SPA changes the boundaries of traditional applications and processes

SPA allows organizations to shift from rigid, generic, developer-centric applications solving one particular problem, to agile, contextual, user-driven applications that support specific business objectives. This eliminates the artificial barriers imposed by the traditional concept of an application or business process. Instead of separating processes from data, functionality and human decision making, they all come together in a single framework.

SPA facilitates emergent solutions

SPA allows users to produce something "good enough" as soon as possible, deploy it immediately, and refine it later if needed. The formal methodology of traditional applications, favoring a "big bang" approach – getting all the requirements, then programming – is unnecessary.

SPA facilitates crowd-sourced development

Using the SPA framework, many people can join in the creation of solutions. With Chatter, it becomes a transparent change management tool for business people. You don't just follow people and records, but you can also follow forms, flows, and database changes. If a change is made, you then have the opportunity to "like" it, comment and make suggestions for further improvement. Truly collaborative solution building is a big step in the way organizations engage in the software creation process, and also in the way applications are managed through their lifecycles.

Sidebar: The real-world basis of SPA

It is not necessary to change. Survival is not mandatory.
–   W. Edwards Deming

SPA works because it is grounded in the way that knowledge workers actually work, rather than the way we think they should work. We always try to make things run like clockwork, but they rarely do. Instead of trying to make the clock work better, we need a more realistic way of looking at the way things really happen.

Flocking birds are an example of Complex Adaptive Systems (CAS). There is no lead bird micro-managing the other birds and telling them all where to fly. The individual birds self-organize by adhering to a few simple rules.

The self-organization leads to unpredictable results; you cannot predict the specific patterns that will emerge, but the behavior is adaptive and highly robust.

In contrast, a large, monolithic production application is a complicated system – brittle, predictable, and hierarchical – requiring detailed planning and control. A CAS is NOT complicated: instead, it is adaptive, non-hierarchical, self-organizing, with robust emergent properties. Simple rules can lead to emergent results.

Applying the lessons of CAS can help us build tools that are more robust, more innovative, self-organizing and can quickly adapt to changes in the environment. Adopting a different frame of reference changes one's perspective so that what was remote and unnatural becomes sensible and natural.

CAS recognizes the difficulty of planning everything in detail, especially when working within an unpredictable and constantly changing environment. It suggests that the best way to plan is by establishing minimum specifications (what coarse-grained steps need to be done?), a general sense of direction (what is the ultimate objective?), and a few basic principles (e.g., how hand-offs take place) on how to get there. Once the minimum specifications have been set, individuals self-organize and adapt as time goes by to a continually changing context.

Order is not preordained before the work begins – it emerges from the interaction of the independent participants through an iterative learning process. Because a CAS can quickly learn and adapt and is capable of efficiently aggregating the collective intelligence of its many participants, it is a far better organizational model for knowledge workers.

Examples of CAS concepts

Sub-optimal: A CAS does not have to be perfect in order for it to thrive within its environment. Any energy spent on being better than "good enough" is wasted energy. Once it has reached the state of being good enough, a CAS will trade off increased efficiency every time in favour of greater effectiveness.

Connectivity: The ways in which the agents in a system connect and relate to one another is critical to the survival of the system, because it is from these connections that the patterns are formed and the feedback disseminated.

Simple rules: Complex adaptive systems are not complicated. The emerging patterns may have a rich variety, but like a kaleidoscope, the rules governing the function of the system are quite simple.

Edge of chaos: A system in equilibrium does not have the internal dynamics to enable it to respond to its environment and will slowly (or quickly) die. A system in chaos ceases to function as a system. The most productive state to be in is at the edge of chaos where there is maximum variety and creativity, leading to new possibilities.

Nested system: Most systems are nested within other systems, and many systems are systems of smaller systems.

Prerequisites for SPA

An effective SPA builder requires two critical prerequisites to be in place.

A complexity shield

For SPA to work, users must be shielded from the ever-growing complexity of enterprise systems. Users can't be expected to understand and traverse the intricacies of legacy systems, and they can't wait around for IT to contextualize these systems for them.

Therefore, users need to access a single business operations platform where they can get the data and services they need in order to collaborate and create solutions quickly with others. This is provided by Force.com.

An actionable activity stream

Since there is no "application" for users to go to, *work must follow the worker*. So each step of a process is triggered at the right time, for the right person, and it shows up in their social network activity stream.

Prerequisite #1: A unified enabling platform that spans the enterprise

In order to truly become a customer company, you need a customer platform - a platform in which sales, service, marketing and applications, even products can leverage shared customer data and processes.
–Salesforce ebook

Cloud computing makes it possible to create new "business operations platforms" that will allow companies to change their business models and collaborate in powerful new ways with their customers, suppliers and trading partners – stuff that simply could not be done before.
-Peter Fingar, *Dot.Cloud: The 21st Century Business Platform*

No matter how good your user development tools are, it's going to be exceedingly difficult to build stable, coherent, efficient and effective software solutions for your organization when your system environment looks like this to business users:

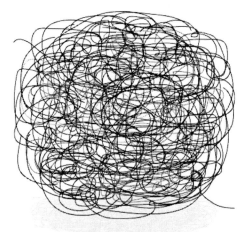

Users need the ability to build processes that are independent of the underlying systems. They need to be shielded by a single business operations platform where they can get the data and services they need when they need them, in order to create solutions quickly with others. SPA needs to have a simple communication and collaboration layer where everyone can interact without regard to the existing systems. The existing systems provide services and data, but they do it through the platform, making it much simpler for users to manage.

Without a complexity shield

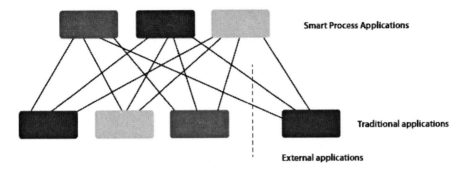

Smart Process Applications

Traditional applications

External applications

With a complexity shield

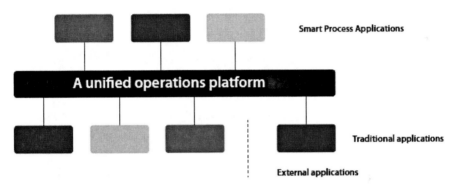

Smart Process Applications

A unified operations platform

Traditional applications

External applications

The foundation

"In the cloud, on the Web, there's no distance to slow us down, no custom infrastructure we have to build, no paperwork to get lost. We can make connections, harness resources and start interacting without ever having to wait for physical stuff to happen first."
– Phil Wainewright, "From Fixed to Frictionless Enterprise," ZDNet

Look at it this way: If you were building a railway, you would need an entire foundation to be built before trains could even think of getting going. This would require a lot of planning up front, construction would be long and complex, and at the end of it all, riders would have to conform to predetermined routes and inflexible schedules. Taxicabs, on the other hand, can be on the road immediately, have completely undetermined routes, and no schedules.

Taxis can do this because the foundation is already in place – roads, traffic lights, gas stations, electric cabling, telephone lines, and so on. This is a vast, interconnected, and mostly unnoticed network that operates to support the business activity.

Taxicabs only have to worry about their business. They don't have to be concerned with building and repairing roads and bridges, installing traffic lights, or monitoring that no one is abusing limits put in place to protect all users. They don't have to provide the services necessary to make it all work, such as traffic cops or gas stations.

To decisively change the application development paradigm, a complete foundation and supporting services must be able to be taken for granted. That is what Force.com will provide you and your organization.

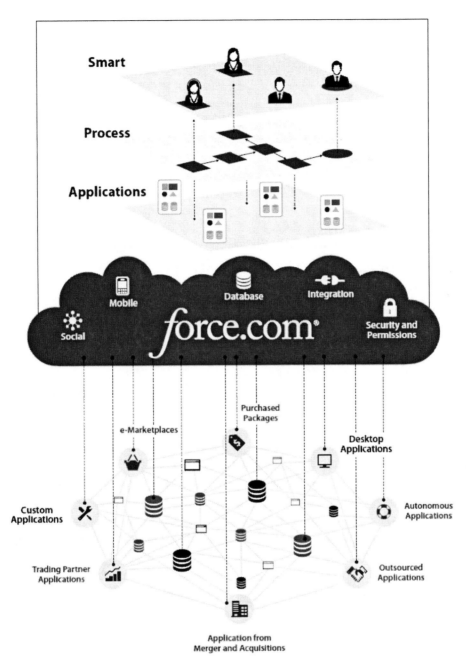

Figure 26: Force.com acts as a complexity shield below, and an enabling platform above.

Platform layers

The unified platform is made up of four key layers: the infrastructure layer, the database layer, the social layer, and the mobile layer. Put together, these layers form a powerful platform that allows users to do complex things, without addressing what makes them complex.

Each layer provides the core functionality that SPA needs to thrive.

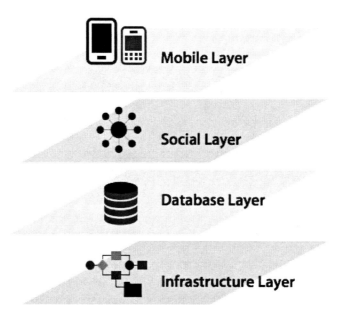

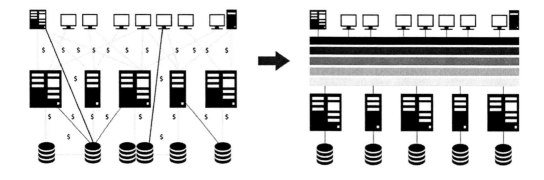

The Infrastructure Layer

SPA is the tip of the iceberg. All the underlying complexities required to support SPA are essentially "below the surface," and must be hidden so users don't have to think about them.

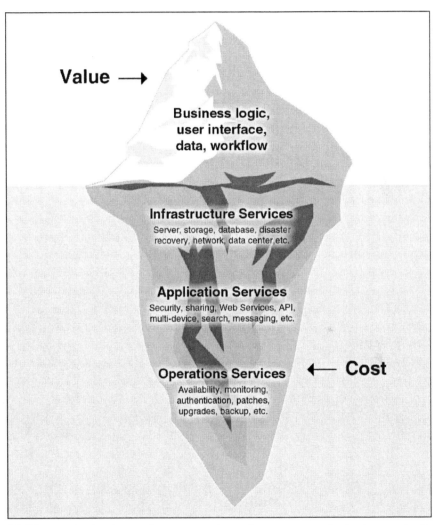

Figure 27: The organization does not have to waste time and resources procuring hardware and software, doing installation and maintenance, and dealing with day-to-day operational tasks in order to implement SPA.

The Data Layer

Most user-developed solutions are at the mercy of their underlying data sources. The data layer makes "businessperson-friendly" data sources and related services available. The data layer simplifies the interface to keep users from getting in over their heads. It is critical for the success of SPA.

Making data easily available to users will make them much less likely to access data sources in ways that are less secure and less accurate.

The data layer brings together, in a single repository, the information needed to build cross-functional solutions. The database reflects the entire extended organization, rather a particular application. It is the anti-silo.

With Force.com:

- **Database management** requires no technical skills, is automatically tuned and optimized, and is highly scalable. There is no low-level management such as patching, backups, or configuration. Reliable and secure, the database is constantly monitored and administered by dedicated professionals whose only job is to manage the database. Databases are instantly available to anyone who needs them with just a few mouse clicks; there's no waiting to provision databases.

- **Data security** rules are isolated and managed independently from the rest of application business logic. This eliminates the need for applications to have to code, test, and maintain their own complicated security logic. Database sharing rules can be defined by user, profile, role, group, and record level. This protects against inadvertently giving the wrong person access to data.

- **Organizational hierarchy** is built into the database. This allows access privileges to be set at different levels of the organization; e.g., a manager can automatically have access to the records of their team members. Yet another complication the solution builder doesn't have to worry about.

- **New systems** can be brought online quickly, because being enabled by Force.com eliminates the steps to acquire, install, and maintain software, and provides immediate access to accurate and complete data in a single location, obviating the need to build new interfaces or cleanse data, or waste effort due to incomplete information or looking for information.

Having the data layer in place provides the additional advantages:

A single data integration point for existing enterprise data, thereby eliminating the need for data duplications.

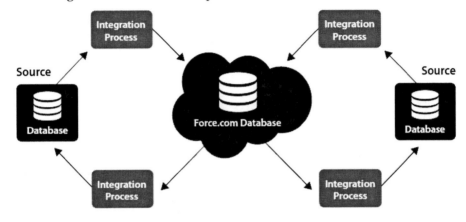

Figure 28: IT gets to do integration just once for all SPA users.

A single, uniform view of data regardless of source from across the organization, giving a consistent context for the use of data anywhere in the organization.

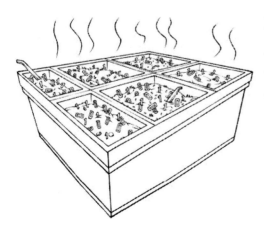

Non-redundant, clean and current data synchronized across multiple business systems that can be used to build solutions throughout the company.

A single place for IT to control data accessibility and security, including filtering or masking data that end users should not have access to.

Self-service functionality that allows business developers to quickly and easily integrate the data they need into the solutions they develop.

A seeded database so new applications can be built faster because the central database is likely to have much of the data needed already in place (e.g., Customer Master, Product Master).

Automatic enforcement of rules by the database for every query, freeing developers from having to code security logic into each application they write against the database.

A single, shared database allows multiple applications to share a single database, eliminating the need to create a database for each application, get separate data feeds, maintain silos of data, etc.

A single, federated, self-service database

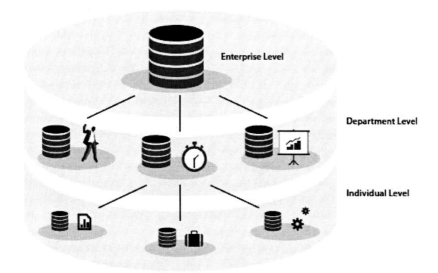

Figure 29: A crowd-sourced, federated database that reflects the organization but provides a way for each business unit and even individuals to have their own data accessible only to them, while still existing in the same database.

The Social Layer

Increasingly, it is becoming clear that the traditional hierarchical enterprise, built on a structure of departments and a culture of compartmentalization, will give way to a socially synergistic enterprise built on continually evolving communities and a culture of sharing and innovation.

—IBM, *The Social Business*

The front office is an unstructured operational area built around people trying to make insightful decisions based on whatever facts are available. In the chaotic, event-driven world of the front office, social networks are the glue that facilitates the finding of alignments between events, people, and data to "organize" collaborative responses to market opportunities. Since the market opportunities are unlikely to align exactly with the way that the enterprise would like to do business, the enterprise has to quickly find answers to all the questions and be "agile" in its ability to match the requirements of the market and its customers in the globally competitive online environment.[11]

The social layer in Force.com is Chatter. Chatter accelerates and improves communication by facilitating direct, unfiltered, unmediated dialogue within the organization, with suppliers and with customers and prospects. The social layer provides a common communications and collaboration channel for everyone in the extended enterprise. Chatter is the primary communications and collaboration channel for SPA.

Chatter helps facilitate SPA in a number of ways:

Engage in real-time collaboration. Users can see when their colleagues are online, instantly chat with them in context and share their screen.

Facilitate the creation of communities that allow users to invite customers and partners to collaborate in private, secure groups.

Kill "Reply all" by allowing a producer of information to simply add the information to the activity stream so that everyone who needs to know about it will be updated immediately - with no action taken on their part, like having to open an email.

---

[11] Andy Mulholland, "2012: the year of unstructured technologies and market change," CTO Blog, January 16, 2012

Get easy access to previous conversations. Find out what was said in the past about a customer, project, step, etc. in one place. This also helps a new team member instantly get access to past and current updates simply by subscribing to the project activity stream.

Allow users to "listen in," eliminating the dreaded infinite email thread. Creating a conversation within the activity stream allows those not directly involved in it to simply "listen in" when needed, giving them the ability to learn, keep track of, and understand what's happening around them so they can better plan for the future, make fewer mistakes, and meet their goals.

Instantly see important changes in your business and collaborate with the right people to take appropriate actions at the right time.

Bridge the gap between enterprise applications and the way people work. Facilitate dynamic, informal, and shared communication within the work context.

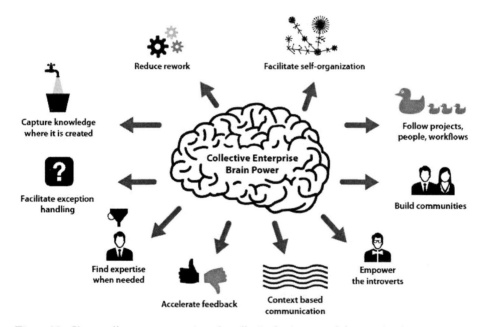

Figure 30: Chatter allows users to tap into the collective brainpower of the organization.

The Mobile Layer

Mobility is all about getting data from point A to point B, and the main challenge lies in the nebulous middle area. The two end points are known (i.e., the back-end host system and a smart phone device), but the in-between contains many unknowns, such as speed of connections, bandwidth, communications protocols, availability of networks, load balancing, and redundancy.

The Force.com mobile layer brings together myriad disparate devices and back-end systems into a unified platform that is simple and manageable for users. It enables companies to standardize on a common framework to ensure rapid deployment, consistent quality, and end-to-end security. The mobile layer provides reliability for mobile apps because all the idiosyncrasies of mobility are seamlessly processed and managed within a unified technology stack, rather than passing through an array of systems and data centers.

On the Force.com platform, users can use SPA to design, build, deploy, and manage their mobile applications across the company.

The mobile layer includes:

Over-the-air management. Users never have to plug in to update administrative information or receive automatic updates.

Centralized administration. Manage users, applications, and devices from a central console.

One platform. Develop and run mobile and desktop apps on a single on-demand platform.

Security. Working over secure layers, with built-in features, such as encryption of transmitted and cached data, robust user authentication and roles assignment, and protection against attempts to access back-end systems, provide the enterprise-grade security that makes transition to enterprise mobility a viable business strategy.

Scalability. Force.com provides the ability to extend mobile apps to millions of users and transactions around the globe.

The power of one

The Business Operations Platform externalizes the control of processes away from individual applications. It makes them equal peers, subjugated to the Business Operations Platform layer that controls the execution of the processes, the provision of services, and the delegation of tasks or activities to the individual applications according to their specific uses and needs.
- Peter Fingar, *The Business Process Platform in the Sky*

Getting everyone on the same platform does not mean that everyone needs to use the platform to build solutions for themselves or their organizations – they can continue using whatever it is they use now (though of course they can also use the platform to build their own solutions). It just means that data and information can be shared easily through a single platform that everyone is connected to.

Having just one platform to deal with allows users across the organization to start building solutions immediately and deploy them quickly, globally, and inexpensively.

Figure 31: You could create your own business operations platform by cobbling together disparate social, mobile, process and cloud products. Or you could simply use the comprehensive, integrated, extensible, and ready-to-go Force.com platform.

It's critical to note that having *a single core platform* is much more important than the bells and whistles it may or may not have. If a car doesn't have all the essential elements that make it run smoothly and make it easy to operate, it doesn't matter if the car has 12 speakers instead of 1, or 1 cup holder instead of 10.

However, the beauty of a platform like Force.com is that if you need those 12 speakers, you can go to the Appexchange and plug them in – much like you can add luxury packages to a car.

The benefits of using a single platform include:

Decreased time to market by eliminating the decision-making process regarding what technology to use, what hardware to procure, and what software to install and maintain.

Long-distance collaboration and support by giving users, developers, and specialists the ability to work from anywhere at any time in one place.

Reduced training and support costs, by making community support more effective with a greater number of participants.

A consistent approach to applications, allowing the organization to benefit from reuse across multiple solutions — reuse of processes, technology, and people and their skills.

The same security profiles and authentication methods are used consistently across all solutions.

A single place for information sharing is provided through a common repository that includes files, content, videos, images, etc.

A holistic view of the organization across applications, departments and information silos is facilitated.

Access to an extensive ecosystem of developers, applications and services that can simply "plug in" to the platform. The ecosystem also reduces the need to reinvent the wheel.

Effective social networking by having everyone on one platform.

A single place for customers to interact with your organization.

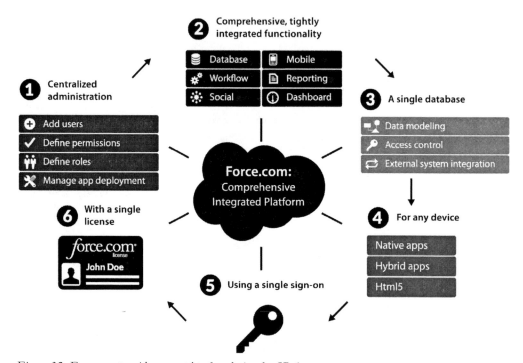

Figure 32: Force.com provides a complete foundation for SPA.

Prerequisite #2: An actionable activity stream in context

Consider the immense benefits of being able to connect all of the elements of your work and your resources in a way that represents the reality of how you experience the world rather than a representation of how your desktop today presents the world to you, in myriad disconnected pieces; broken chains of conversations, information and process.
-Thomas Kouloupoulos, Chairman Delphi Group

In the desktop days, users used Windows and applications to help them contextualize their work. This was fine then, but not now.

Following the worker in the activity stream

The need to take action comes to users in their activity stream. This puts the user in the center of their own workflow. Each process has its own activity stream, but each user only needs to see the pieces that apply to them, thereby improving their attention allocation.

Since there is no "application" for users
to go to in order to do their work, *work
must follow the worker.*

When the task arrives in the user's activity stream, it comes with context and it is actionable; i.e., the user can take action on this piece of work directly from their activity stream.

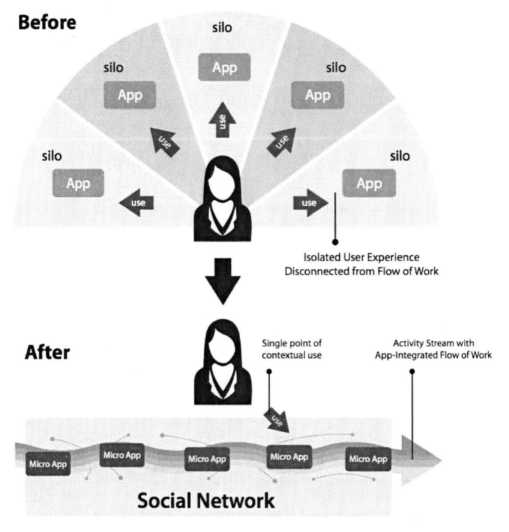

Figure 33: Micro-apps become part of the social layer, in the user's Chatter feed, and the user can collaborate and take action directly from within their activity feed.

Since workers are usually working on multiple processes at the same time, having work come to their activity stream provides them with a single point of access for them to do their work.

This allows workers to interact as they normally would in the social environment, and process steps simply appear as another interaction type, and can be done within the flow of their day.

Adding context to the activity stream

When the action surfaces in the activity stream, it comes with enough information and context, including data, comments and documents, to help users successfully complete the required activity without leaving their activity stream.

This leads to information being captured as it is created. Any information related to the action taken by the user is captured and stored within the context of that action, so that it is there for later use as well as to provide an audit trail and for process improvement.

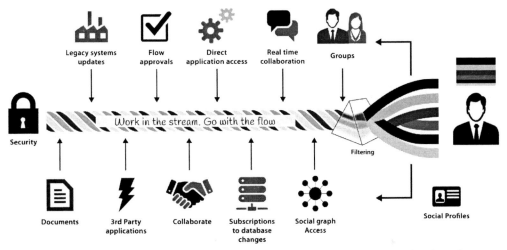

Figure 34: Instead of the user going from application to application to complete their tasks, the tasks appear in the user's activity stream as needed. For example, a manager needs to approve an expense report: instead of going to the expense reporting application, the request will simply show up in their activity stream, along with any associated notes, attachments, and a direct link to the record being acted upon.

Process visibility in one place

The activity stream allows a user to see a process in its entirety. For example, if a manager needs to approve a service request, instead of going to the service management application, the request will simply show up in the manager's activity stream, along with information about the state of the process, as well as any associated notes, actions, or attachments, and a direct link to the record being acted upon.

Tacit knowledge mining

The importance of tacit knowledge is growing rapidly because all knowledge is time-sensitive – shelf life is limited because new technologies, products, services, regulations, etc., continually pour into the marketplace. Knowledge of yesterday's "best practices" may not help with today's or tomorrow's problems. Rather than having explicit knowledge at your fingertips, it becomes much more important to know *who* knows something when you need it.

Chatter allows workers to reach out to a large number of relevant participants and bring them into a virtual discussion around a specific problem or challenge, so tacit knowledge is shared and new knowledge is created. Chatter captures these informal conversations, and makes them searchable, rather than leaving the answers to important questions in your head or in your email.

Documents and files in motion

Users can also move documents and files into the activity stream so that instead of having different versions on each person's computer, there is only one version available. When it is updated, everyone concerned will be notified. Chatter provides a single, consolidated space to find all the information and communications you need.

The time dimension

The timeline of a process is visible from within the activity stream, making it easy to, for example, plan ahead, understand how long a process is taking, and see why the process is behind.

Bypassing email

The problem with email is that the information it spawns is lost, buried, or out of context in the bowels of the email system. For example, an email exchange about a project may not be tied directly to the project, making any information the email contains difficult to find or reuse for similar projects. If you forget to click reply-all, people are left without key details they need to move forward, and if you accidentally hit reply-all, people are inundated with more knowledge they don't need. It can be difficult to find specific emails when you need them, if you're even able to remember which information was contained in which email.

With so many emails floating around, it's impossible to stay on top of everything. As a result, it's easy to miss crucial information, such as a new product update, or a requested delay for an order shipment when a critical customer update is missed.

By using Chatter instead, all conversations related to a specific process or task within the process will be easy to find.

Providing automatic status updates

When work is automatically tracked in the activity stream, there is no need to send regular status updates to your team when an action is completed – those who need to know about it will know and they will also be informed of the next steps that need to be taken. If a question needs to be asked about a certain action, it can be asked as a comment, and forevermore linked to that action in case it needs to be referenced later.

Since everyone with permission, including customers and partners, can monitor the status of a business process's progress through each and every stage, workers can avoid callbacks and unnecessary escalation, while speeding up requests for additional information.

Taking action from inside the activity stream

The activity stream becomes actionable in the sense that users can take actions within the context of the activity stream – instead of going to different applications to get different tasks done, all applications aggregate within the activity stream and tasks can be completed right from the activity stream as they come up.

> Process steps simply appear as another interaction type in the worker's activity stream, allowing them to take action within the flow of their day.

So when a worker needs to respond to an item in the activity stream through an application, they don't need to toggle away to the application.

For example, if an approval is required, the worker can execute the approval by clicking a button to approve or reject the request without leaving their activity stream. Instead of going to an application and navigating it to do what they need to do, they are told that there is a task assigned to them, and are then provided with the functionality they need right in the activity stream. This way, users can close the loop on the step they are responsible for without leaving their activity stream.

The anatomy of a Smart Process Application Builder

The health, competitive power, and even survival of an enterprise largely depends on its ability to understand and harness the power of knowledge workers who are enabled to take responsibility for providing automatic solutions to meet many of their business needs.
– IBM System Journal, *SOA meets situational applications: Examples and lessons learned,*

A SPA Builder is a comprehensive, integrated, cloud-based framework for knowledge workers to build their own process-driven solutions.

It is designed in a way that allows users to start building their solutions immediately, much like they would fire up an Excel spreadsheet – nothing needs to be done in preparation before starting.

Familiarity with just the basic concepts are enough to get started – no manuals, and definitely no training classes. The framework ensures that many of the common pitfalls of process and software development are avoided.

Deployment to multiple users is simple and immediate. Users can start getting real value out of the system immediately.

Desktop Software **Cloud Software** **On-premise Software**

Figure 35: SPA builds a layer over the fragmented systems that make up every organization.

Complete Visibility

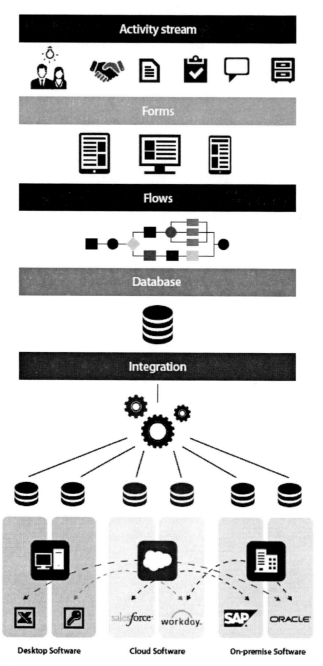

Figure 36: By providing a business operations layer on top of the organization's fragmented systems, SPA provides a holistic view of processes.

The SPA builder creates the organization's playbook

In the future of work, employees must be empowered to operate at their full potential, and this requires a workplace that has freed itself of unnecessary and debilitating boundaries. It is only then that companies can hope to meet the business challenges of the fast-changing global economy.
– Cognizant, *Future of work enabler: Worker Empowerment*

A SPA is like an overall game plan in football. As in any sport, rather than trying to define all the ways the game will be played, you outline the properties and behaviors of the players and systems so they know how to behave when different "plays" come up. Things can be changed on the fly if necessary, and approvals, cooperation and exceptions are built into the process.

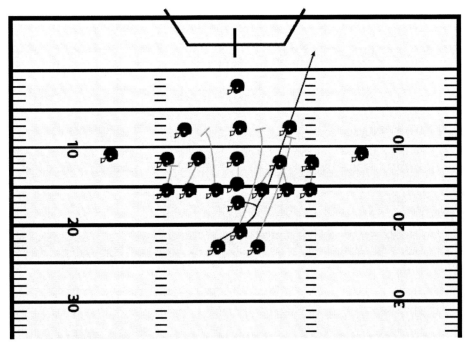

Figure 37: A playbook spells out the roles, responsibilities, and expectations for every participant, and lays out all the possible activities, paths, and resources.

The game plan (*process*) determines:

- Plays (called *flows*) that can be executed in the pursuit of the game plan objective.

- Individual actions (*steps*) that need to performed by each player (*participant*) within each play.

Individual players are responsible for executing their step in the play in a defined sequence.

Sometimes the play will break down due to unforeseen circumstances, in which case the players need to improvise. This improvisation may lead to a change in the play for when it is run in the future, or perhaps added as a new play that can be made part of a future game plan.

The benefits are obvious:

- Breaking the game plan into plays provides the coach (*process owner*) great flexibility in planning and executing the game plan.

- All team efforts are focused toward the team's common goal.

- Measurements are made on the common result – the one that counts.

- The functional breakdown – quarterback, linebacker, safety – is subordinate to the common process.

- *Who* fulfills the function doesn't matter to the planning, and can be substituted at any time – like bringing in the backup quarterback when the primary quarterback gets carted off the field.

- The plays allow for unique circumstances, like a hurry-up offense that requires the elimination of certain routine steps, or calling an audible to take advantage of situational opportunities or challenges.

If the framework provides a "rulebook" that will clearly spell out who does what, what everyone's expectations for them are, and how the company defines acceptable behavior, it will be easy for everyone to follow. Essentially, you can tell employees, "How you do your job is not my concern as long as it gets done correctly."

Overall architecture

Agile systems are actually quite simple. Complexity is a trap. In a world that is constantly changing, complex systems become harder and harder to change. If you come up with these kludgy systems, you're toast. You'll never catch up. You might keep up for the first six months, but after that the system's a boat anchor.
-Michael Hugos, *Agile BPM for improved business agility*

A smart process application is built to address a specific business objective, like manage a project or job, handle a service request or customer complaint, handle an event, or implement a procedure. It is built on top of a unified platform or layer, like Force.com.

Every process application has one or more flows. The process application is simply a container for any number of interrelated flows.

Figure 38: An application consists of one or more processes, which contain one or more flows, which contain one or more steps.

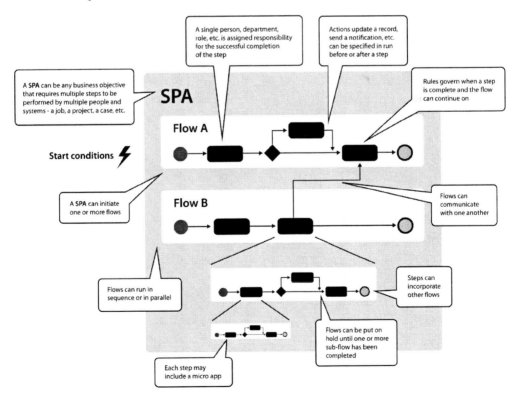

Flows

We must learn to cocreate the future and use an improvisational model for strategy that embraces uncertainty, emerges from execution, engages individual creativity and learns by testing many hypotheses.
- Mike Rollings (Gartner), *Citizen Development: Reinventing the Shadows of IT*

A flow takes on the role of a play in a game playbook in that it is a scenario mapped out by the participants in the play. Once the scenario is established, the participants are identified, and the steps required to meet the objectives of the scenario are defined at a high level.

The sequence of the flow is determined by who needs what, and when, to get their piece of the flow done. *How* each step is completed is left to the individual participants. They may use the functionality provided by the SPA builder to complete their steps, or they may identify some external system to provide the needed data and information, or they may do it manually, perhaps with a spreadsheet, then key it in.

Once a flow is activated (the play is called) and triggered, participants are notified through the activity stream when it is their turn to complete a step.

Each subsequent step in a process is determined only by the outcome and other circumstances of the preceding step. In addition, there may be unanticipated parallel activities that occur without warning, and may have also an immediate impact on the process and future (even previous) activities.

Characteristics of SPA flows

Design by doing, not doing by design
- Gartner, Social BPM: Design by Doing

Flows are emergent. They don't need to be fully designed in advance – they have the ability to be changed and adapted on the fly. The system captures the flow as it unfolds and provides the option to make it a template for future processes with the same characteristics.

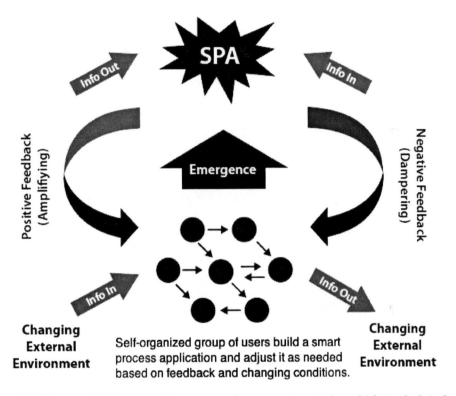

Figure 39: Emergence is the way complex systems and patterns arise out of a multiplicity of relatively simple interactions.

Flows are adaptive. Users can turn past executions of a process into new or improved processes that incorporate things learned along the way, so users have an easier time reaching their target the next time.

Flows are expansive. Rather than seeking to *constrain* the resources available to people, flows strive to continually *expand* the choices available, while at the same time helping people to find the resources that are most relevant to them.

Flows follow the worker. Flows tell users and systems when it is their time to do something. Flows can make sure that all your upcoming tasks are on a worker's radar – the system will automatically check active flows and update the worker via the activity stream if they are responsible for the next step.

Workers can create "just-in-time" processes. Users can combine pre-built flows with other pre-built flows to quickly create solutions and adjust to new situations.

Rules ensure compliance and policies. Rules can ensure that certain flows cannot move forward without express approval, or without prerequisites being satisfied. Human judgment, embodied in a "Proceed" button, can override the rules. Users can optimize their flows at any time, while respecting corporate compliance rules.

Flows provide visibility. Management and workers can see what is happening in real time through dashboards linked into the flow data.

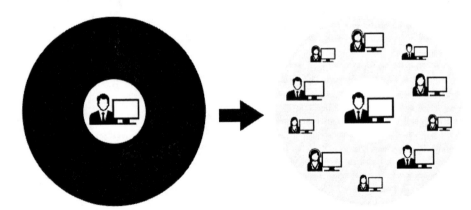

Figure 40: Individual workers toil in the dark, with no visibility into the work of others. Flows shine a light on overall processes.

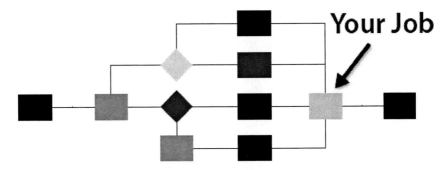

Figure 41: Workers can easily see where their work fits in with everyone else's.

Flows facilitate hand-offs. Flows ensure that the handoff of work between employees, departments, and organizations goes smoothly, reducing the risk that key pieces of context and information are lost in the transition. Flows can also automate the transfer of work where appropriate, ensuring that co-workers can respond quickly and everyone is kept apprised of the work that must be completed.

Flows can be changed on the fly. Users can easily modify processes as they occur, by adding or deleting steps or changing how they fit together.

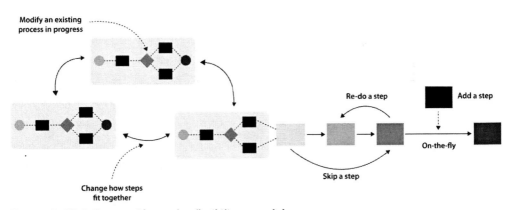

Figure 42: SPA flows provide complete flexibility as needed.

The Flow Builder

The Flow Builder is a visual drag-and-drop canvas that makes it easy for users to create and modify flows.

The Flow Builder provides the ability to design a basic flow quickly, with very little investment by the participants. All users must do is:

1. Create placeholders for each step
2. Connect the steps with flow lines
3. Add any necessary decision gateways
4. Add basic user interfaces
5. Run the flow

The user can deploy a high-level view, and the details can be filled in later, by adding rules, actions, sub-flows or checklists (which may later become sub-flows). The user can continue to add more sophisticated functionality slowly, as they begin to better understand how things work and what is available. Since they already have a working solution, they can experiment with new functionality in a meaningful way.

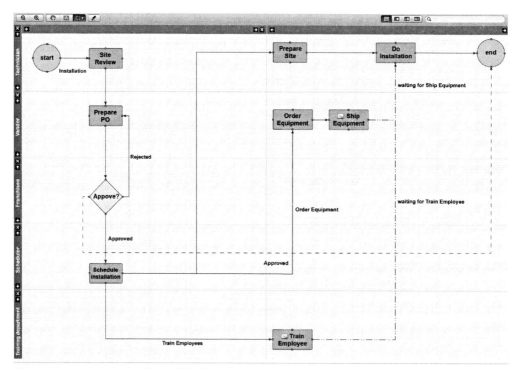

Figure 43: An example of a SPA builder. Note that there are just a few step types – there is no learning curve to overcome to start using the builder.

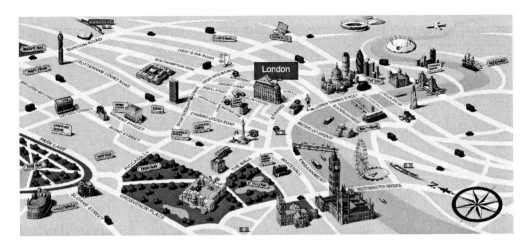

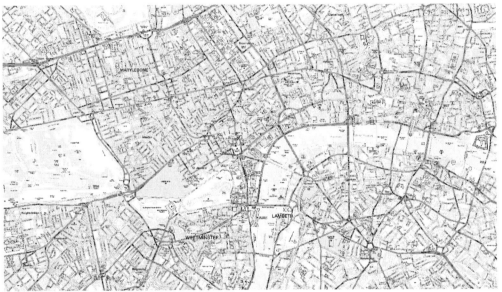

Figure 44: *SPA allows participants in a process to start with broad brushstrokes, and define details as needed.*

The Project Management View

Instead of using the visual editor to define steps and connect them using drag-and-drop, it is sometimes easier to simply create a list of nested tasks with responsibilities and durations. This is especially useful when sequence is not overly important. These non-linear, activity-based solutions require a different perspective.

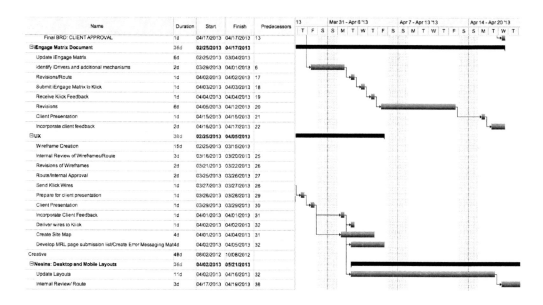

Name	Duration	Start	Finish	Predecessors	13	Mar 31 - Apr 6 '13	Apr 7 - Apr 13 '13	Apr 14 - Apr 20 '13
Final BRD: CLIENT APPROVAL	1d	04/17/2013	04/17/2013	13				
⊟iEngage Matrix Document	38d	02/25/2013	04/17/2013					
Update iEngage Matrix	6d	02/25/2013	03/04/2013					
identify iDrivers and additional mechanisms	2d	03/29/2013	04/01/2013	6				
Revisions/Route	1d	04/02/2013	04/02/2013	17				
Submit iEngage Matrix to Klick	1d	04/03/2013	04/03/2013	18				
Receive Klick Feedback	1d	04/04/2013	04/04/2013	19				
Revisions	6d	04/05/2013	04/12/2013	20				
Client Presentation	1d	04/15/2013	04/15/2013	21				
Incorporate client feedback	2d	04/16/2013	04/17/2013	22				
⊟UX	38d	02/25/2013	04/05/2013					
Wireframe Creation	15d	02/25/2013	03/15/2013					
Internal Review of Wireframes/Route	3d	03/18/2013	03/20/2013	25				
Revisions of Wireframes	2d	03/21/2013	03/22/2013	26				
Route/Internal Approval	2d	03/25/2013	03/26/2013	27				
Send Klick Wires	1d	03/27/2013	03/27/2013	28				
Prepare for client presentation	1d	03/28/2013	03/28/2013	29				
Client Presentation	1d	03/29/2013	03/29/2013	30				
Incorporate Client Feedback	1d	04/01/2013	04/01/2013	31				
Deliver wires to Klick	1d	04/02/2013	04/02/2013	32				
Create Site Map	4d	04/01/2013	04/04/2013	31				
Develop MRL page submission list/Create Error Messaging Mat	4d	04/02/2013	04/05/2013	32				
Creative	48d	08/02/2012	10/08/2012					
⊟Nesina: Desktop and Mobile Layouts	38d	04/02/2013	05/21/2013					
Update Layouts	11d	04/02/2013	04/16/2013	32				
Internal Review/ Route	3d	04/17/2013	04/19/2013	38				

Figure 45: Users can start building complex processes by simply entering a nested task list. Project management "tasks" are the same as process management "steps," allowing the user to toggle between the two views.

So instead of using a flow view for activity-oriented solutions, users can manage the associated tasks from a project perspective. Here the focus is less on the flow, and more on the tasks to be completed in a time-sensitive format, while still allowing relationships and interdependencies on those tasks to be displayed in a visual format.

To facilitate this, the Flow Builder allows users to toggle between a visual flow and a corresponding list view. The list view is called the Project Management View because it looks and works exactly like the interface you find in a project management tool like MS Project. Users can start by creating a simple list, and the Flow Builder will transform the list into a flow. Users can then add precedence, rules and actions using the flow view.

Using the project management view, if a certain task is taking longer than planned and will throw off the timeline, the business user can easily modify other tasks to bring the process back in line to successfully meet the deadline. This simple approach allows a project manager to complete a project effectively in the face of the changing demands of the situation.

The Flow Folder

Human judgment about the advancement of the SPA frequently depends not on a single document or activity in isolation, but on the collection of process documents, tasks, and data as a whole. Thus, all SPA information – subject to security and access control rules – is simultaneously available to all users working on the case through the shared flow folder. In addition to data and documents, the folder provides shared access to case tasks, deadlines, notes, completion status, and an audit trail.

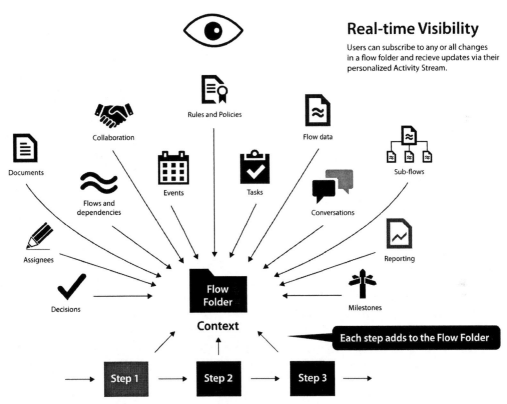

Real-time Visibility

Users can subscribe to any or all changes in a flow folder and recieve updates via their personalized Activity Stream.

Rules and Policies

Collaboration

Flow data

Documents

Sub-flows

Events

Tasks

Flows and dependencies

Conversations

Assignees

Reporting

Decisions

Flow Folder

Milestones

Context

Each step adds to the Flow Folder

Step 1   Step 2   Step 3

Figure 46: The flow folder accumulates everything related to the flow as it progresses. The combination of flow folders in a process represents the complete picture of the process.

The Flow Library

Flow snippets

The SPA builder easily facilitates the ability of users to quickly add small flow segments to a process. The flow library contains ready-made flows that can be added to a new or existing process as required; e.g., there may be a flow for referral to a loss adjuster or fraud department that needs to be added to a specific instance of a process.

Flow templates

Users can create a template from a successfully completed flow and clean it up for universal application (all non-essential discussions and comments are deleted; only important assignments and control points are kept). As a result, for each subsequent flow that has the same or similar characteristics, there is a convenient template with a list of tasks, assignments, rules and conditions: documents to use as a starting point. Now a new instance of the flow can be created with a single click. The ever-increasing library of flow templates composes corporate knowledge, separated from individual employees and stored in digital format for corporate use.

Flow Rules

There are sometimes things that can't be changed, like breaking the law by going faster or ignoring other rules of the road.

SPA provides mechanisms to selectively restrict change to flows. With the potential for serious missteps in the execution of flows, organizations need the balancing capability to lock down certain steps in their flows, ensuring compliance on the one hand, enabling goal-centric behavior on the other. This provides flexibility while still ensuring control where variations are not permitted[12].

Many complex systems are based on simple rules. A set of several simple rules leads to complex, intelligent behavior, while a set of complex rules often leads to dumb and primitive behavior. There are many examples of this.

Flocking geese follow a simple set of rules when flying in formation: don't bump into each other, match up with the speed of the other geese flying by, replace the lead goose when it gets tired, and always remain with the group.

---

[12] The Forrester Wave: Dynamic Case Management, Q1 2011

From these few simple rules, a complex and efficient flying pattern emerges.

The point is that flow rules are used sparingly in SPA compared to what you would find in traditional BPM. There is no attempt to nail down each possible path or every possible exception. This provides the individual participants a large degree of autonomy, while reaching the group's objective efficiently under many different circumstances.

There are 3 types of rules that can be included:

Hard rules

These are rules that can't be broken or require extraordinary authority to override them. These are often used to enforce compliance requirements, for example. Going back to our football analogy, these would be the rules of the game.

Soft rules

Soft rules are designed to steer users in the right direction. They are more like suggestions that ultimately get enforced based on user judgment. These are the plays where participants are expected to keep within the bounds of the play formation.

Sequence rules

These rules ensure that a step cannot start until the prerequisites for starting the step can be met; e.g., the quarterback can't throw the ball until the receiver is in position. You can't ship an order until it is complete, or until the buyer's credit has been checked. Sequence rules can be hard or soft.

The function of rules

- Rules ensure that flows do what they are supposed to do.

- Rules determine the path a process should take based on different conditions.

- Rules constrain the selection of specific tasks, or trigger other tasks and flows based on the user's selection of tasks within a flow.

- Rules can be used to determine when a task can be marked as complete, when a task can be started, when exceptions need to be processed, etc.

- Rules ensure compliance with regulations, security and policies.

- Rules provide a full audit trail of what was done by whom, where and when.

- Rules provide an element of consistency.

Flow Actions

Actions make it easy for users to build complex solutions without having to write any code. Actions can easily be added to a process using the Flow Builder.

Pre-defined actions include:

- **Send email:** You can create pro-forma emails to be sent, along with whom they should be sent to and when.

- **Create issue:** You can alert the appropriate employees that a problem has come up and needs to be resolved.

- **Create, update and delete records**

- **Callout:** You can trigger a web service or APEX code for additional functionality.

Users can execute actions based on conditions when a task is started or when it is complete.

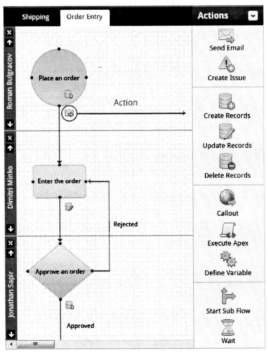

Figure 47: An example of SPA actions. Note that the number of actions is limited, but action properties provide users with a significant amount of functionality without having to resort to callouts or APEX execution.

Steps

> *The trick...is to introduce bits of automation that will fit into the work and do useful things, and then make it possible for people to work with those bits of automation embedded in the systems while leaving them the discretionary space to exercise the kind of judgment they need to exercise to really get the work done.*
> - Derek Miers - Process Innovation and Corporate Agility (2007)

A step is a unit of work; it identifies an activity or task(s) that needs to be done before the flow can move forward. Steps are explicitly defined and operationally independent units of functionality. Each flow consists of multiple steps, and a single step can be in multiple flows.

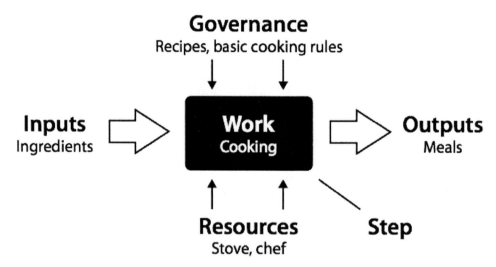

Figure 48: A step is a complete unit of work[13].

---

[13] Adapted from Alexander Samarin.

Pre- and Post- Step Conditions

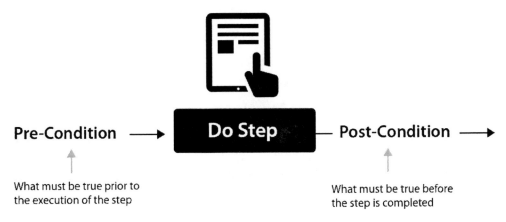

Pre-Condition ⟶ **Do Step** — Post-Condition ⟶

What must be true prior to
the execution of the step

What must be true before
the step is completed

Figure 49: A step is not executed until its pre-conditions are met, and is not completed until it satisfies the rules for completion.

Pre- and Post- Step Actions

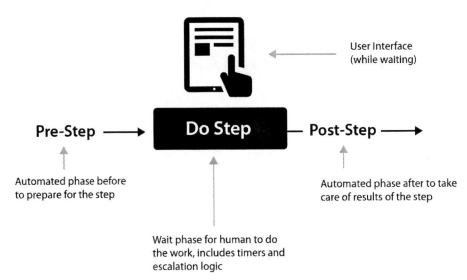

User Interface
(while waiting)

Pre-Step ⟶ **Do Step** — Post-Step ⟶

Automated phase before
to prepare for the step

Automated phase after to take
care of results of the step

Wait phase for human to do
the work, includes timers and
escalation logic

Figure 50: The objective is to surround a step with as much automation as possible to help a user complete the step as quickly as possible.

The ultimate goal is to ensure **success at every step** by empowering the person responsible in every way possible.

Pre-Step

The goal of pre-step actions is to reduce the amount of work a human has to do to complete the step by preparing as much as possible in advance. This means making sure that all the data, documents, and information are ready to go.

Post-Step

The actions taken during the execution of the step, including any decisions, collaboration, documents, etc., must be complete before the step can be accepted as complete. Upon completion, the system will execute any actions specified.

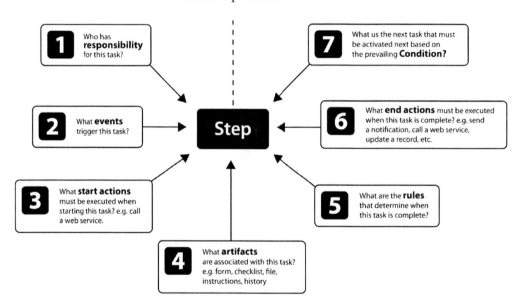

The step repository

Each step in a flow includes a step repository, which provides the context needed to determine what happens next in the flow. It helps the flow participant responsible for the step to accurately assess the state of current affairs and their impact on downstream steps and what needs to be done now to accommodate likely events in the future.

Anything related to a particular step that may be helpful in the future can be stored in the step repository. This can include a form built by the user responsible for a step, a set of guidelines and checklists, comments from users of this step, discussion notes, optional sub-flows, task lists, documents and files, past discussions around this step, as well as a full history of decisions made at this step and why they were made.

Adaptability requires the ability to accurately assess the full and relevant context of the current status.

The step repository also provides a container for capturing implicit rules and tacit knowledge, and is enormously helpful in resolving problems and exceptions quickly.

The repository contents are changed and added to as needed. Where a decision needs to be made, the repository includes data regarding the choices that were made previously, and why.

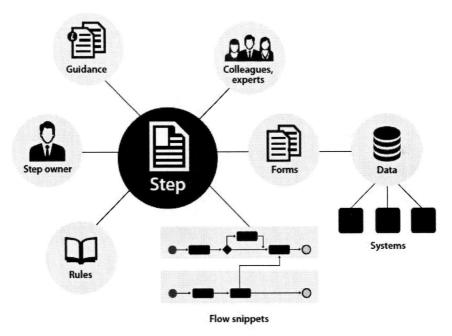

Figure 51: Everything needed to execute the step successfully is available in the step repository. The unique information related to each individual execution of the step is also stored in the repository, and provides an audit trail of that flow instance. The step repository provides information used to monitor the flow (like expected time to complete) and for analysis across multiple executions.

Characteristics of Steps

Step initiation depends on prerequisites being satisfied
A step doesn't get initiated until all the prerequisites are satisfied (though this can be manually overridden by clicking a "Proceed" button and giving a reason). A step doesn't get started until someone has been notified that it needs to be done.

Steps surface in the responsible party's activity feed
Instead of the user going from application to application to complete their steps, the steps appear in the user's activity stream. For example, if a manager needs to approve a service request, instead of going to the service management application, the request will simply show up in their activity stream, along with any associated notes, attachments and a direct link to the record being acted upon.

Steps can be adapted to the prevailing conditions
The sequence in which a step is executed, and the rules by which it is governed, can differ from flow to flow and flow instance to flow instance. Users can spawn additional steps as they are being performed – these can be assigned to someone else and must be completed or canceled before the parent task can be completed.

Steps include just-in-time guidance
Employees need information quickly - they can't wait for colleagues to email them back and they may not all be in the same office to speak in person. Acquisition of knowledge in a fast-paced, complex world becomes less important than the ability to search, create, and manipulate information to generate knowledge on demand and just-in-time learning. The best way to visualize this is to recall the movie *The Matrix,* in which revolutionaries trying to free an enslaved human race are hard-wired for data downloads. When in need, characters bark out their knowledge needs to colleagues who download the appropriate information – from driving directions to kung fu.

Guidance can be localized for different languages, and improved on the fly, as the instructions are being given. Poor guidance can make a simple task hard to perform, while great guidance can simplify a complex task.

Steps are a focal point of collaboration

Change is the organizing force, not a problematic intrusion.
- Margaret J. Wheatley, Finding Our Way: Leadership for an Uncertain Time

The step is a collaboration hub. Worker's tasks almost always have the potential to become collaboration tasks, because performing them raises questions that other people have to answer – meaning someone else has to supply information before the task can be completed. By facilitating direct, unfiltered, unmediated dialogue within the organization, between suppliers, and with customers and prospects, the organization's responsiveness enhances its reputation and prospects.

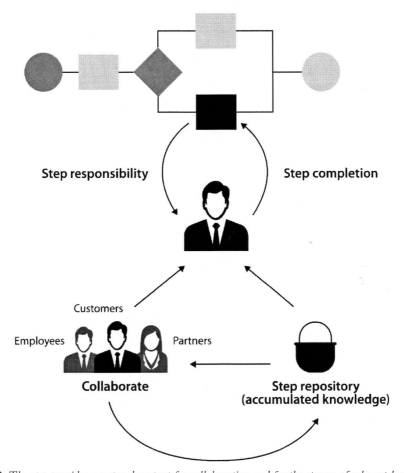

Figure 52: The step provides a natural context for collaboration and for the storage of relevant knowledge.

Steps provide context

Context drives the process, and a different context results in a different process. The participant responsible for a step will have all the information related to the task at hand available at their fingertips. They will know about special circumstances, previous conversations about the topic, and even the analytics from prior, similar decisions. Having all the information about the steps in a workflow allows users to see what decisions have been made in the past, and what the results of those decisions were.

> A process is context aware when it is capable of responding to changes in the environment, based on rules and conditions, in real time.

Steps facilitate exception handling

When an exception needs to be handled at a step, the exception can be dealt with in three ways: they are either detectable, unknown, or resolvable.

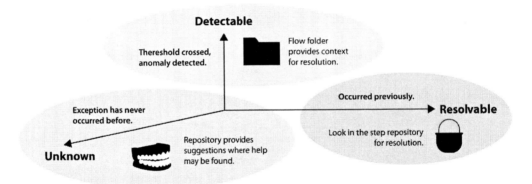

Figure 53: When an exception occurs when executing a step, the user is provided with multiple tools to help ensure the fastest path to resolutions.

A single, explicit entity is responsible for a step

Every step has an identifiable person or entity responsible for it. This includes users, groups, roles, etc. Assignments can be made manually, or users can be automatically drawn from resource pools as defined in the assignment rules. This capability allows just-in-time resource allocation, enabling a more accurate view of enterprise resource utilization in real time.

Step Issues and Checklists

A checklist might be the best way to model complex, unstructured ad-hoc processes. When a process is not predictable, putting a lot of work into an elaborate diagram is not worthwhile.

Checklists can be incorporated into each step so that no task, no matter how small, is forgotten about. You can create rules so that until each box on a list is checked, the workflow cannot move forward.

Additionally, users can create dynamic checklists based on what has occurred previously. Issues that have come up repeatedly with a step can be noted, along with a sub-checklist of what the user must do if such an issue arises.

Notifications, reminders, escalations

At each step, a user can establish conditions under which notifications should be sent and to whom; establish multiple reminders based on the step duration (e.g., send a reminder after 5 days, 10 days, etc.); and define the rules for escalation, including the timing of the escalation and the person who will receive the escalation message.

The person responsible for a step can also set up reminders for themselves. The reminders will pop up in their activity stream.

Forms

SPA does not require a fancy and finely tuned user interface (UI). Since the UI is in the activity feed, this is especially true. It requires an effective UI that can quickly be adapted when the process needs to change.

When the issue of UI is taken out of the equation, it becomes very easy for non-tech users to create their own forms.

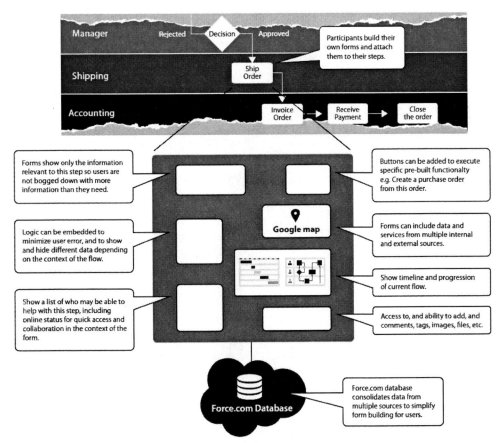

Figure 54: Forms are the user interface of the step. The form can be as simple as an Approve/Reject button, or as complex as the example above.

The Power of Composite Mobile Applications

Business value increases exponentially when companies implement mobility strategically across an entire organization, rather than as a one-off or point solution. The potential of mobile will be realized in a composite fashion because mobile applications will integrate multiple enterprise systems, legacy systems, and third-party content with inherent device capabilities (camera, phone, GPS) and unified communication (UC) technologies such as presence (knowing if someone is online and willing to communicate) and instant messaging (IM). Mobility brings everything together in a meaningful, relevant way and enables employees to work smarter and faster than ever before. Mobile can have an explosive impact with context-aware composite applications and composite transactions, based on the notion that one mobile action can spawn myriad business reactions — yielding returns exponentially higher than the initial mobile investment.

Characteristics of forms

Designed for the user, by the user

Participants in a flow can create their own forms. The forms reflect specifically, and only, what the user is tasked with accomplishing at that particular point in the flow. Participants, given appropriate rights, can modify the forms and business logic embedded in the forms on the fly, if needed.

Minimalist

Forms reflect the most granular piece of information that is needed to complete a step. The objective is to provide simple features and functions with pre-populated data that make it as easy as possible for users to complete their step. To be effective, forms (just like mobile apps, which they will often be used as) need to be highly targeted and often single-function. The fanciness of the form is much less important than its ability to guide users through their tasks with a minimum amount of keystrokes and mouse clicks.

Provide a micro context for collaboration

The form itself can be used as a hub for discussions related to the step; i.e., collaboration can be initiated and conducted within the form. Additional steps can also be added from the form; e.g., if it is decided after collaboration that an approval for a proposed solution is required.

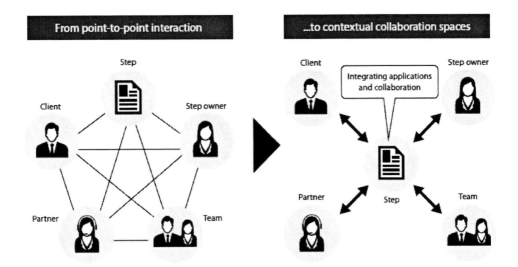

Provide a composite view

Forms provide a real-time single, uniform view of data regardless of its source from across the organization, giving a consistent context for the users of data anywhere in the organization.

Embed external system user interfaces

In some cases, especially where people use a high proportion of an application's UI, the best solution may be for users to continue to use the application directly. Force.com Canvas provides this capability.

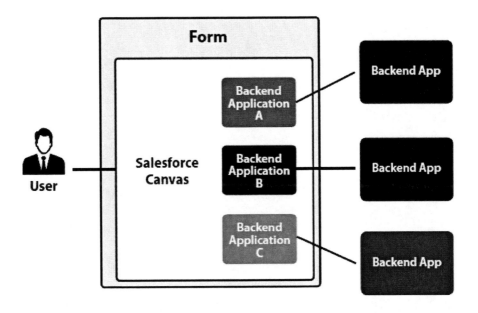

Immediate deployment

Forms can be built quickly and deployed immediately by the step owner, with no intermediate steps required.

Device presentation

The form is created once, and is automatically adapted to the device on which it is rendered.

Validation rules

Each field in a form has its own validation rule. Collections of fields may have interdependencies. Rules that are applied may be changed as the process progresses and depending upon who is manipulating the field.

Time

Process flows show a general sense of time (left to right or top to bottom), but there is no visual indication of duration – all steps are the same size.

On the other hand, project management tools like Gantt charts are good at representing a flow timeline, but poor at facilitating workflow.

A time view of flow

SPA provides a time dimension based on the step's responsibilities, durations, and precedence. SPA fuses project management methodology with a process management interface. It enables users to create and quickly implement non-linear business processes that include many interrelated tasks and dependencies. The web-based interface enables business users to create and model processes through a project management interface, with no coding.

Milestones

Since processes are emergent, visibility and control can only be achieved in the context of the process instance by monitoring the process as it executes and enabling the process owner (or anyone else permitted) to view the current and past states of the process. Monitoring provides details on both the emerging flow of the process (the hand-offs between participants) and the work done by each participant (in either summary or detail form).

Since the process is defined as it executes, the only way to determine that the process is stuck is that a deadline has been missed. Therefore, there clearly is a need to measure and predict the time it takes for a workflow, and each task, to be executed. This can be done through the use of milestone markers.

Events

An "event" is literally anything that happens that can impact the way a case is handled. Events are captured as they are happening so that workers or the system can react to them as they occur.

SPA allows users to define conditions under which an event triggers a step or workflow. This includes complex events, comprised of related individual events, which traditionally go undetected because they have multiple characteristics and may occur at different times spanning geographic locations.

SPA allows processes applications to subscribe to multiple events, thereby allowing the organization to immediately respond to opportunities and problems as they occur.

Unpredictable events can have a major impact on tasks to be done and flows in process. SPA facilitates the definition and monitoring of potential events, as well as the actions to be triggered when an event occurs. This could involve things like:

- Starting up a new flow, either automatically or as a result of human decision making.
- Modifying a currently active process, like canceling some steps, or adding or activating new steps.
- Suspending or canceling an active process.
- Initiating a compensating process to unwind steps affected by the response to the event.

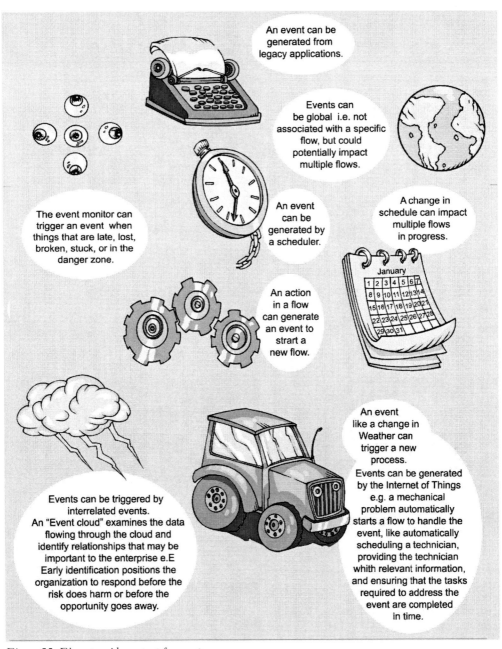

Figure 55: Flows provide context for events.

Monitoring and Analytics

Monitoring

Monitoring allows users and systems to see what is happening in real time. SPA allows for the consolidation of monitoring, reporting, SLA escalations and the creation of an audit trail.

With monitoring, users can get a sense of what flows are currently in process and where they are in the process, if there are any problems with impeding flows, if the ball has been dropped along the way, etc. Managers can determine how busy their staff is at any given time, and whether anyone needs assistance. It can eliminate the necessity of the dreaded status-update meeting or conference call by allowing anyone with permission to check on a process at any given time.

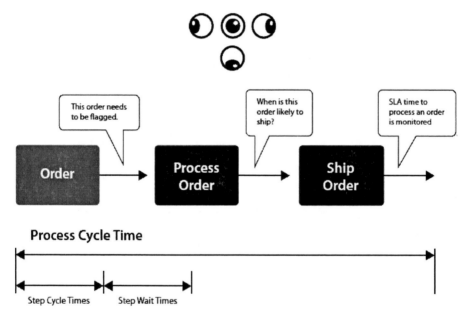

Figure 56: Monitoring and analytics work together. Analytics provide the data, like threshold limits, needed for monitoring.

Analytics

Once a process is complete, users can benefit from analysis provided by the SPA. Through both monitoring and analytics, they can answer questions like:

- How long does a flow typically take to complete?

- Where are the bottlenecks?

- Why is this flow taking longer than expected?

- What is the current value of active flows?

- How many flow instances are currently at this step in the flow?

- What is the threshold for days overdue?

- What is the average time it takes a flow to move through these steps?

- What tends to cause a flow to be blown off course?

Patterns

Analytics can be used to take the data accumulated through monitoring and look for patterns that can be used to improve processes.

For instance, if a particular step took three days on average to complete, the system automatically knows to recommend a due date that is three days after the task is activated. Users can always choose to reset or override these alerts and notifications if necessary.

Service Level Agreements

Users can predict missed SLAs by comparing history to the activity timeline in order to estimate overall time to completion. For example, if multiple shipping agents are available to deliver a shipment, and one of them continuously fails to meet SLAs, thereby affecting customer satisfaction levels, you can model a flow so that if a shipping agent continues to miss SLAs, future shipment requests are sent to an alternate agent.

Best next step

SPA analytics can help users make decisions when presented with a set of optional steps based on an analysis of the decisions previously made during the execution of the step.

Users can drill down on each option to see the circumstances that led to a successful outcome in the past. The system can also suggest an option by analyzing the conditions of past selections.

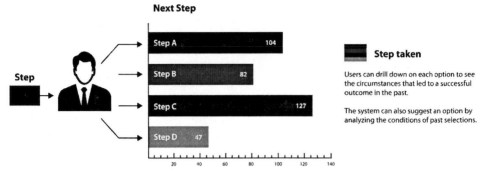

Figure 57: Analytics help users select the appropriate response based on past results.

Other possibilities with SPA analytics include:

Analytical triggers. For example, spawn a fraud-detection process when a series of events occurs for a customer.

Find potential problems. Locate anomalies before they become problems.

Understand root causes. Identify the underlying problems instead of immediately visible symptoms.

Achieve compliance. Uncover non-compliant situations and incidental non-compliance that would otherwise be impossible to locate.

Compare performance. Compare departments or similar organizations based on verifiable data, not hunches.

Validate process changes. Establish baselines for the current situation and use them to determine whether specific changes are effective or not.

Understand the entire process. Departments often focus on completing their own subtask, unaware of the complete chain of actions that bring a product or service to the customer.

Gain transparency. Once the causes of problems are identified and seen in the context of the organization's overall workflow, users can understand where and why change is needed.

An efficient early warning system. Stop reacting after the fact by seeing critical KPIs (quantity, time, cost and quality) in real time — and even predict potential outcomes.

Faster and better decisions. Identify process deficiencies more quickly, and take immediate corrective action before things get out of hand.

Dashboards and reporting

The results of monitoring and analytics can be displayed on the dashboard and used for reporting.

Trends and traffic lights can be used to visualize the performance (cost, processing time, and so on) of activities.

Analytics Dashboard

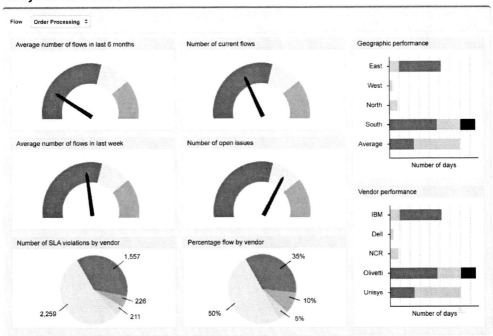

Process status dashboards are provided for users who "own" some operational aspect of a process. For example, if a supervisor is responsible for the completion of specific processes, the supervisor can see the current status of all the running processes, with those processes highlighted that are at risk of not being completed on time.

Users can initiate action from within their dashboard. For example, a user could initiate an escalation process or reassign some of the tasks to other participants without leaving their dashboard.

A process status interface also provides estimates on when specific process instances may be completed based on the remaining steps that must be performed and estimates for how long each step is expected to take.

Company Dashboard

Filters

Flow [Order Processing ‡] Milestone ‡ Step ‡ User ‡

Flow	Record	Description	Current Step	Issue Status	vs. Average	SLA Status	Flow
Order processing	Order #4251	Taco Bell Tacos	Manufacturing	▬		▬	▬▬▬
Order processing	Order #1235	Wendy's Burgers	Shipping		▬		▬▬▬▬▬
Order processing	Order #4556	McDonals Buns	Waiting approval				▬

Issues

[New Issue]

Action	Subject	Category	Priority	Assigned To	Lock Workflow?	Status	Created Date	Created By
Edit | Del	Training Material	Training	High	Fred Jones	Yes	▬	Jan 3, 2013	System
Edit | Del	Equipment Late	Vendor	Med	Jim Smith	No		Jan 4, 2013	Sammy Sosa
Edit | Del	Manual Missing	Help Desk	Low	Jane Mack	Yes		Jan 5, 2013	Help Desk

Figure 58: The company dashboard provides a snapshot of all the processes currently in progress, with the ability to filter and drill down as needed.

User Dashboard

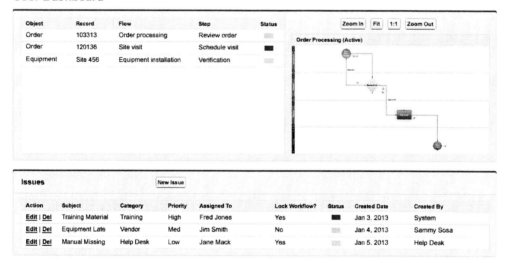

Object	Record	Flow	Step	Status
Order	103313	Order processing	Review order	
Order	120136	Site visit	Schedule visit	▬
Equipment	Site 456	Equipment installation	Verification	

[Zoom In] [Fit] [1:1] [Zoom Out]

Order Processing (Active)

Issues

[New Issue]

Action	Subject	Category	Priority	Assigned To	Lock Workflow?	Status	Created Date	Created By
Edit | Del	Training Material	Training	High	Fred Jones	Yes	▬	Jan 3, 2013	System
Edit | Del	Equipment Late	Vendor	Med	Jim Smith	No		Jan 4, 2013	Sammy Sosa
Edit | Del	Manual Missing	Help Desk	Low	Jane Mack	Yes		Jan 5, 2013	Help Desk

Figure 59: The user dashboard provides each worker with a list of tasks behind schedule, in progress and on the radar. The worker can also see visually where their task fits into the current process flow.

Extending SPA with code

It is true that there often will be the need for some coding to complete a robust SPA. Therefore, it must be easy for IT and business developers to work together collaboratively to reach their goals.

Figure 60: SPA allows an ever-increasing amount of a solution to be built with clicks. When clicks are unable to provide the functionality required, code can be written and slotted in. SPA makes this seamless through the use of Force.com APIs and development language support necessary for developers to extend and enhance the platform with new services and capabilities that meet the specific needs of your business.

SPA provides a bridge for users and IT developers to actively participate in building the code needed. The idea of the "bridge" is simple – when you clarify the role of IT and the role of the business developer, and provide a clean line between the two roles, the SPA framework acts as a bridge.

Each role owns part of the solution. SPA manages the contract between parties to ensure that neither side can break the other's work. The result is that both are free to be agile in how they work together to achieve their goals.

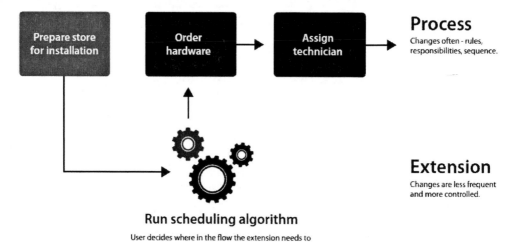

Process
Changes often - rules, responsibilities, sequence.

Extension
Changes are less frequent and more controlled.

Run scheduling algorithm

User decides where in the flow the extension needs to take place. The developer doesn't need to understand the entire context of the application.

Figure 61: With SPA, many of the difficult issues typically faced by coders are resolved (architecture, methodology, patterns, etc.) and there is no "classic" application – instead, there is a set of orchestrated steps.

Sidebar: For the IT sceptics

Normal people can and will innovate of their own initiatives if
enabling conditions are present.
–A. Van de Ven, *The Innovation Journey*

The reason big new things sneak by incumbents is that the next big thing always starts out being dismissed as a "toy." This is one of the main insights of Clay Christensen's "disruptive technology" theory, which observes that when a new product or service is introduced, it is dismissed as a toy because when it is first launched it undershoots user needs, but then tends to get better at a faster rate than users' needs increase. How mainframe companies viewed the PC, or Kodak viewed digital cameras are obvious examples.

There is always great skepticism (admittedly justified, for the most part), especially on the part of IT, about whether end users are capable of developing their own applications beyond some spreadsheets and Access databases.

But this time it's different. We have reached the perfect storm of conditions that will transform the landscape for end user application development.

Lowering the barrier

Given an appropriate set of tools and services, technically savvy
business users can build situational applications by themselves.
- Mike Rollings (Gartner), *Citizen Development: Reinventing the Shadows of IT*

Lowering the barrier to building solutions will make more people programmers – but not in the traditional sense. You could say there are now fewer typists and switchboard operators than there were in the '80s. Technically, that's true, but it misses the bigger picture.

Nowadays, we're all "typists" and "switchboard operators" to some degree – but our new tools and what they make available have opened up tremendous new possibilities. The same is true of software solution building.

Consider drones.

A drone "pilot" needs many fewer qualifications to operate a drone than a pilot has to fly a jet. Yet a drone today can accomplish much of what a fighter jet can accomplish – with much less training and a lot less effort.

How? By dramatically simplifying what the person has to do to accomplish an objective.

Drone technicians are never going to become fighter jet pilots. Just because they can take off and land, do aerial surveillance and fire a missile doesn't mean they are capable of becoming jet pilots. The whole point is that, given the right tools, the drone technician doesn't ever *have to* become a pilot in order to achieve a significant sub-set of the functionality required by an experienced pilot.

Interestingly enough, jet pilots are unlikely to become drone technicians either – the air force has found they have much better success when they take someone "off the street" and train them to pilot drones. Which makes sense – the technicians want as much done for them as possible, while the jet pilots are used to having complete control. It's not easy to make the switch. That's why a Java programmer is unlikely to start building smart process applications.

Factoring in Millennials

An important scientific innovation rarely makes its way by gradually winning over and converting its opponents.... What does happen is that its opponents gradually die out and the growing generation is familiarized with the idea from the beginning.
-Max Planck, *The Philosophy of Physics*

While end-user application development has been around for a long time, we are entering into a whole new phase of citizen developers. This is the result of the entry of Millennials (roughly, people born anywhere from the late '70s to the mid '90s) into the workplace.

When computers were first introduced into the workplace, they were viewed as mysterious and intimidating. Users learned the functionality by rote, and never strayed from what they were taught.

For the most part, the way we build information systems today still assumes a workforce that is computer-illiterate. Users must be provided with everything they need and are given little opportunity to create their own solutions (other than standalone desktop applications for private use).

Now, however, we're seeing a much more computer-literate worker – and even the older workforce is becoming more IT savvy and capable of more than they are given credit for.

The Millennials flooding the workforce have different expectations, skills, and values. After all, they are the first generation to grow up with IT as an integral part of their environment. Members of this tech-savvy generation unveiled the mysteries of technology at an early age and are adept at using it. They will not think twice about provisioning, configuring, and developing business applications.

In the end, companies that cater to the mobility and social media cravings of millennials stand to gain an innovative mindset that will surely shape their future.
- Cognizant, *Tapping the Elusive Millennial Mindset*

Many of the tech-savvy business developers' supervisors are Millennials themselves, and therefore encourage business developers to find faster ways to get business done. Users have always been tempted to bypass backlogged IT developers, and their tech-savvy supervisors are even less tolerant of hearing that IT can't get to their project for months, if ever.

Millennials are also familiar with common development metaphors. Their broad use of applications has made them familiar with data relationships, visual design, and interactions with applications. They can use this as a base of knowledge when designing their applications.

Elimination of infrastructure requirements

Perhaps the biggest barriers to end-user development have finally been eliminated:

- Getting a budget to procure hardware and software
- Installing, maintaining, scaling, upgrading and performance tuning
- Creating backups and planning disaster recovery
- Managing security and permissions for every solution

This makes it far easier to start new projects quickly and keep them running without regular maintenance and extra staff.

Pre- data integration

The goal is to provide users with a comprehensive, clean and current set of data that they are able to use to build their solutions. Not having to waste time looking for data, getting data feeds set up, and ensuring the data they have is pristine, goes a long way toward facilitating the rapid development of user-developed solutions.

Taking advantage of micro-apps and orchestration

Before mobile, if you wanted to create an application, you needed to understand a lot about databases, application architecture, security, etc. Everything had to work with everything else for the application to function correctly, and a change in one part of the system could seriously impact another.

Now, with micro-apps and their orchestration, there is much less that a user needs to understand to build a meaningful solution, and these solutions are isolated through the framework from stepping on other parts of the system.

Leveraging social networks

The social network provides users with access to a treasure trove of useful information and the ability to easily find snippets of functionality that they can include in their solutions, and makes it easy to find assistance from co-workers and external users of the platform. The social network also facilitates the joint development of solutions among users across the globe.

Facilitating the inclusion of code

SPA eliminates many of the traditional problems experienced when users and developers attempt to work on the same applications. There are very clear boundaries between users and developers in the SPA framework, preventing them from stepping on each other's toes. There are very clear places in a flow in which externally developed code can be slotted.

There is the added advantage that the developer does not have to understand the entire flow to develop some code. The developer also does not have to be concerned with the architecture of the application, or dealing with security and permissions.

Figure 62: The SPA framework ensures that users don't hit a wall by facilitating the addition of code in the context of the framework.

The role of IT with SPA

Clearly, it's time for IT to dramatically extend its capabilities and reinvent itself. No longer is it enough to just meet the current needs of the business; IT needs to position itself as the enabler for continual adaptation of the corporate operating model to ongoing waves of change.
- Cognizant, *The Future of Work Has Arrived: Time to Re-Focus IT*

The role of IT in the enterprise is rapidly changing. The mix of IT resources and roles will change dramatically over the next few years. Rather than something negative, SPA should be seen as an opportunity to better serve the business.

While it is entirely possible for individual business units to implement SPA on their own, it will be much more effective if IT is involved.

CIOs have an important but challenging role: to change the enterprise culture to one that encourages and embraces innovative thinking and individual self-sufficiency. They need to actively remove existing technological and cultural barriers to support an entrepreneurial atmosphere.

Time is of the essence. The longer you delay, the more entrenched business units will be in their chosen technology, and the chances of bringing them back into the fold will rapidly diminish. Now is the time to act, and SPA with Force.com provides the solution IT needs to get started.

The following are some of the ways IT can be effective with SPA.

Embrace SPA

Embrace Shadow IT. Shadow IT is a gift. It's the business telling you what they want.
- Drue Reeves, Gartner vice president

Citizen developers are here to stay and will fundamentally change the future of IT work. How you embrace them will determine the future of IT within your organization and define the role IT plays in the creation of new innovative business practices.
– Mike Rollings (Gartner), *Citizen Development: Reinventing the Shadows of IT*

It is becoming easier than ever for a business to procure cloud-based services without IT involvement. If IT doesn't add value, business units will simply work around it, and that would lead to a much smaller and less impactful corporate IT resource. On the other hand, by working with users to provide them with an effective way to develop and deploy solutions, IT can greatly expand its reach and enhance its value.

SPA provides opportunities for IT to:

- Service low-end, disenfranchised users;
- Provide an effective way to tackle high-value back-burner issues and alleviate the IT bottleneck;
- Help restore the luster of the IT department by allowing them to quickly and effectively deliver customized solutions;
- Make IT a business innovation partner, delivering a competitive advantage to the business; and
- Move IT beyond being an operational cost center, into a business growth enabler.

The thought of giving business users the ability to do things themselves may seem like a big leap. But in the same way that outsourcing a spreadsheet to IT is absurd today, so too will outsourcing many business process applications in the future.

Provide lightweight governance

End-user application development (EUAD) is nothing new, but the risks and opportunities it presents have become much greater in recent years.
-Ian Finley, Gartner research VP

IT needs to ensure that compliance rules are being enforced, that confidential data is not being exposed by users building flows, and that agreements with third-party asset providers are enforced.

The risks posed by user solution development has grown significantly, because instead of individuals building applications for themselves and their workgroup, the power of SPA means that users can now build departmental, enterprise and even public applications.

Build a Rapid Response Center

IT provides frameworks, tools and environments for use by the citizen developer, and IT works with citizen developers to create cooperative relationships to safeguard and use data.
– Mike Rollings (Gartner), *Citizen Development: Reinventing the Shadows of IT*

IT should spearhead the creation of a Rapid Response Center. This is an excellent way to serve the needs of many users with minimal resources, and allow IT to maintain a modicum of control. IT can also accelerate the exploitation of SPA and help end users create competitive advantages and build closer links with their business peers.

The SPA analyst

Ideas for new solutions will spring from half-baked applications created by lay users who may start down the path toward a solution, but may lack the expertise to finish it.
–Mashup Corporations: The End of Business as Usual, Andy Mulholland, Chris S. Thomas, and Paul Kurchina

There are going to be times when users need someone with analyst skills to help them better define a complex process. There are also going to be times when IT or third-party developers will need to be engaged to code some specific functionality for a process.

This is the role of the SPA analyst.

An SPA analyst helps translate a user's requirements into SPA terms, model the data needed to support the application, and help translate complex business logic. The SPA analyst works with IT on behalf of users to secure access to corporate data as needed, and to work with users to write specifications for custom functionality.

The Seed-Evolve-Reseed Cycle

An important aspect of the emergent methodology is the idea of seeding. The analyst would work with users in the following way:

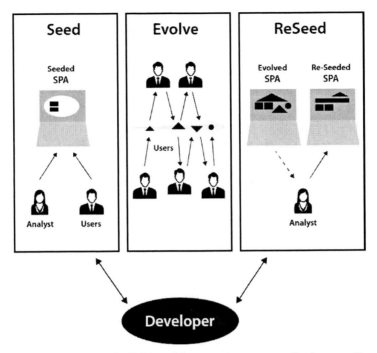

Seed	Evolve	ReSeed

Figure 48: The Seed-Evolve-Reseed (SER) model ensures the process application gets off to a good start, and then is kept on track as it evolves.

- The analyst would basically **seed** the application with the user, helping the user put the first version in play.

- The user(s) would then **evolve** the application any way they like.

- There may be a point during this evolution where the analyst needs to get involved once more to **reseed** the application. Reseeding is necessary when evolutionary growth is no longer proceeding smoothly. It is also an opportunity to organize, formalize, and generalize information and application functionality created during the evolutionary growth phase so that it can be found and shared with others. [14]

---

[14] Daniela Fogli, Elisa Giaccardi, and Gerhard Fischer, "The Seeding, Evolutionary Growth, Reseeding Model," Center for Lifelong Learning and Design, UC Boulder.

The best solutions will ultimately emerge from these small steps forward, with the "final" step representing the sum total of accumulated reseedings.

An SPA Community

To contend, IT must find new methods and structures to enable business growth and sustainable competitive advantage, as new opportunities and ways of working emerge.
- Cognizant, *The Future of Work Has Arrived: Time to Re-Focus IT*

The Center should create and participate in a Chatter community for SPA users.

The community allows users to contribute their knowledge and expertise, and becomes a dynamic repository for information that can be reviewed as needed.

Gamification within the social network can be used effectively to recognize the contributions of users to the repository of knowledge, and for their assistance to others in the community.

Formal recognition of user SPA development will go a long way toward bringing user development up from the underground. When users see they are recognized, they are encouraged to share their knowledge and ideas.

Development services

Inevitably, there will be times when additional functionality is required to support a process, and code needs to be written. IT can either provide the resources to do the programming, or assist users in finding and managing third-party developers.

In addition, when custom code can be generalized for use by others, IT can add it to a centralized functionality repository that can be used through the SPA framework by any user.

Seed the database

All [citizen developers] need are services that can supply them with data to feed these tools. IT can facilitate their efforts by supplying data services that virtualize complex data sources.

- Mike Rollings (Gartner), *Citizen Development: Reinventing the Shadows of IT*

When a user wants to build a SPA solution, chances are they need access to data that already exists – accounts, products, transaction history, etc. SPA solutions that rely on existing data can be built much faster when a base inventory of reliable enterprise data feeds is pre-established so the data can be consumed and mixed as needed for a process.

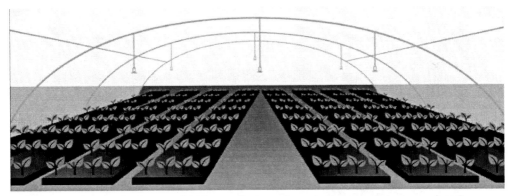

Figure 63: Seeding the database is a highly cost-effective and practical way to eliminate or reduce the amount of time users need to spend to find the data they need, and the need to make requests to data owners and/or IT.

Seeding the database can happen gradually and organically over time, with input from across the organization based on current needs. Crowdsourced seeding promotes cooperation amongst employees to get the best possible seedbed of data.

Once this database has been created, it can function as a "single source of truth" for the organization, for any application. As each record is changed, that information will become available immediately to everyone in the organization with permission to see it – users avoid wasting their time searching for information. Reports can be generated across many different areas of your organization.

Done properly, the database starts reflecting a consistent, cross-functional view of the enterprise. The ultimate goal is to create a single database with no duplication of data that can be used to build all SPA solutions in the organization. There would be one point of control, one system of record, and one place to get reliable, up-to-date data.

This also eliminates the need to download data to Excel or Access, and allows the organization as a whole to drive down the costs of integration and bring new services and products to market faster.

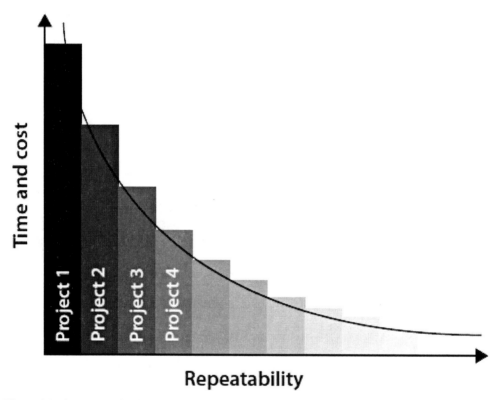

Figure 64: As time goes by, fewer and fewer new sources of data need to be added at the start of a solution, because chances are the data the user needs is already available.

Sidebar: SPA Design Principles[15]

If about everything top-down fragilizes and blocks antifragility and growth, everything bottom-up thrives under the right amount of stress and disorder.
- Nassim Nicholas Taleb, *Antifragility*

The objective of SPA is to systematically reduce the downside from unstructured processes, while at the same time increasing the potential upside.

In his book *Antifragility*, Nassim Nicholas Taleb describes how volatility and unexpected events lead to learning and growth, to become even better as a result of the exposure and experience. This is the essence of *antifragility*, a term Taleb coined to describe the properties of adaptive or evolutionary systems that become better and reach even higher levels of performance as a consequence of encountering and overcoming challenges. These systems are dynamic rather than static; they thrive and grow in new directions rather than simply sustain themselves; they actually need random events to strengthen and grow and they become brittle and atrophy in the absence of these random events.

For SPA to be antifragile, it needs to adhere to some basic principles:

1. Stick to simple rules
Complex systems do not require complicated rules – in fact, the simpler the rules, the better. Resisting the temptation to respond to complexity with complex rules is critical – they have a disturbing tendency to produce cascades of unintended consequences.

2. Decentralize
Decentralized systems are far more antifragile than very large, centralized systems. They are better able to learn from randomness because adverse impacts are contained, and decentralized units can watch and learn from each other as each unit improvises in response to unexpected events. Centralized systems are fragile because they make rules that, by necessity, are more abstract and theoretical so that they can be broadly applicable, but at the same time they are removed from the relevant social context.

---

[15] Adapted from *Getting Stronger through Stress: Making Black Swans Work for You*, John Hagel

3. Resist the urge to suppress randomness

Don't try to eliminate volatility or unpredictable disruptions to a process. The paradox is that efforts to eliminate randomness only intensify the vulnerability of systems to damage from disruption. Without an element of randomness, there can be no serendipity.

4. Ensure everyone has skin in the game

Participants must face the consequences of their actions and endure failure as well as enjoy success. This will ensure that each participant will be motivated to learn as rapidly as possible and not take unwarranted risks.

5. Design by doing

Practice and experimentation drive advances in knowledge and well-being. Instead of analysis and research driving practice, practice leads to analysis and understanding.

Benefits of SPA

The effect of these continuous adjustments and enhancements to business operations can generate a steady stream of savings and new revenues that may sometimes seem insignificant from one month to the next, but as years go by, they become analogous to the growth of capital over time due to the humble but powerful effects of compound interest. The profits generated this way can be thought of as the agility dividend.
- Michael H. Hugos, Derek Hulitzky, *Business in the Cloud: What Every Business Needs to Know About Cloud Computing*

With SPA, it is possible to address unique business challenges without a huge outlay of money and resources. It is affordable, quick to implement, offers easily measurable ROI, and involves far less risk than many of today's enterprise applications. SPA can do this by using modularity to reduce the complexity that occurs when one tries to coordinate large numbers of diverse participants.

The ability of SPA to power your Customer Company is immense. Organizations can find hundreds of ways to make small, continuous adjustments and provide value-added services that will increase their profits and decrease their costs every day, every week, every month.

The Agility Dividend
Agility creates a competitive advantage

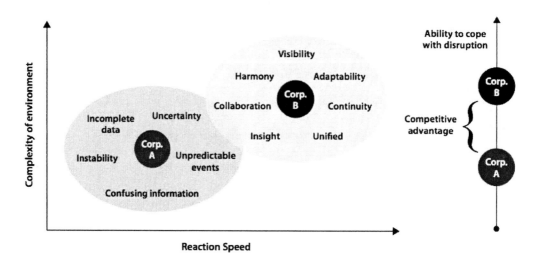

Figure 65: The ability to cope with disruption in an increasingly complex world opens up a significant competitive advantage (adapted from "Business Mashups or Mashup Business?", Peter Evans-Greenwood, Capgemini).

Competitive advantage

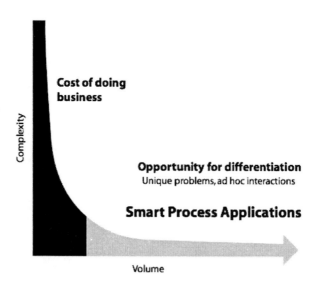

Figure 66: The many every day activities provide the opportunity to make a difference.

Improve efficiency

- **Simplified work environment**. SPA addresses organizational gaps, making operating processes clearer, simpler and automated. SPA makes work easier and saves time, for employees and for their line of management. And with more efficient processes and higher customer satisfaction, managers will have fewer problems to deal with.

- **Increased employee satisfaction**. With SPA, people know clearly what's expected from them and understand how what they do impacts company goals and performance. It gives their job more meaning, while also helping them to manage their time and their daily tasks.

- **Improved customer interaction**. Workers can serve customers more efficiently with less stress and more ownership, thanks to clear processes, computer - aided task management and reminders.

- **Freed-up time**. By eliminating unnecessary work like status meetings, following up, etc., workers are freed up to do productive activities, add value and interact more with their coworkers and customers.

- **Improved data capture**. Building Force.com applications that are specific to the type of data being entered, how it is being entered, and by whom it is being entered can ensure that it does not have to be re-checked later in the process, will not cause unforeseen exceptions later on, and will not have to be re-keyed into other systems.

- **Routine work automation.** Human-centric processes can be streamlined, with mundane and repetitive steps automated and tasks such as milestone monitoring handled by the system. This leads to measurable improvements in process speed, customer response times and overall effort.

- **Captured and shared process knowledge.** A process can be modeled and shared, thereby avoiding knowledge loss when employees change and facilitating the training of new staff. Lessons learned from previous iterations of a process can be captured and made available for subsequent reuse.

- **Reduced response times.** By providing users with a real-time view of process status, they can react quickly to important internal and external events.

- **Improved collaboration**. Collaboration is much easier, so users can share information or initiate discussions on particular stages in a process.

- **Reduced paperwork.** SPA can reduce paper-intensive tasks, thereby freeing users from managing large amounts of paper forms and records.

- **Reduced complexity**. SPA shields users from the complexity of the underlying systems so they can spend more time on productive work.

- **Holistic business processes.** SPA allows processes to be built across applications, departments and information silos.

Improve exception handling

- **Designed from the outset to handle exceptions**. Instead of treating exceptions as indications of failure and spending considerable effort trying to eliminate exceptions, SPA assumes exceptions are a normal part of the process.

- **Immediate exception notification.** Alerts can be sent when an exception is detected, either automatically or manually. This alone can improve the speed with which exceptions are handled.

- **A home for resolutions.** Steps create a permanent "home" for exception handling. Exception management through SPA gives management clear insight for handling these exceptions. Storing the actions taken to resolve exceptions within the step can lead to better implementation, revisions, or training, and increase productivity throughout the enterprise. This also reduces employee burnout by eliminating the need to deal with the same exception over and over.

Improve decision making

- **Faster access to information**. SPA delivers the right information to the right person at the right time.

- **Shared information**. SPA provides shared, common access to the latest information at all times, ensuring that decisions are made using the right information.

- **Consolidated information.** SPA automatically consolidates information from multiple sources into a single repository.

- **Situational awareness**. SPA ensures employees are aware of pertinent information at all times through their activity feeds. This allows them to keep track of what's going on around them so they can figure out the best course of action and are not surprised by events.

Reduce errors and improve compliance

- **Cleaner data.** SPA reduces the need to re-key information by providing single data entry facilities for multiple processes.
- **Intelligent data capture.** SPA provides the user with the ability to create web and mobile forms for intelligent data capture, thereby reducing the need for paper forms.

- **Self-service.** SPA allows the sources of information to enter information themselves (e.g., customers can enter their own service requests) through any device.

Increase customer satisfaction

- **Customized solutions**. SPA facilitates the building of customized solutions, thereby improving customer loyalty by making the client feel you care specifically about *their* unique needs, and by providing them with the ability to help themselves.

- **Faster response.** SPA helps identify problem trends early by automating data monitoring of customer-related activities, and responding faster to customer queries by making information easy to find.

- **Improved communication.** SPA keeps customers informed through automated notifications and increased visibility into processes that impact the customer.

Increase competitiveness

- **Manage the extended organization.** SPA makes it much easier to coordinate and manage outsourcing, virtual teams and business networks.

- **Facilitated innovation.** SPA promotes innovation by empowering users to build their own solutions, and provides more time for innovation by automating common tasks. SPA also makes it easier and less costly to try new services and processes.

- **Increased agility.** SPA allows users to dynamically assemble new solutions and bring them to market quickly in response to changing conditions.

Reduce cycle time

- **Improved visibility.** Improve visibility of commitments so decisions aren't delayed due to missed commitments or poor coordination.

- **Reduced miscommunication.** SPA keeps track of accurate information, making it always available, and making changes immediately visible.

- **Improved work relay.** SPA helps prevent things from falling through the cracks by improving the visibility of commitments and by automating the notification of missed deadlines. This significantly reduces the chance of requests languishing in email boxes and on voicemail systems.

- **Reduced lag time.** SPA automatically notifies the next person in a workflow to start a process (e.g., once a warehouse employee marks all items in an order as received, it comes up in the Chatter feed of the delivery scheduling department, allowing them to start processing the order immediately, without human intervention).

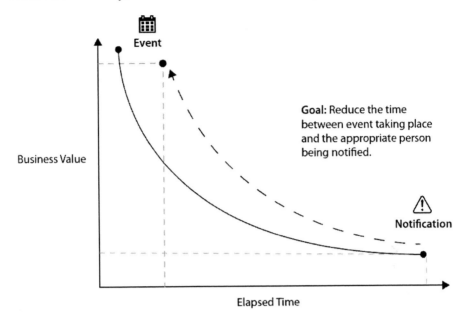

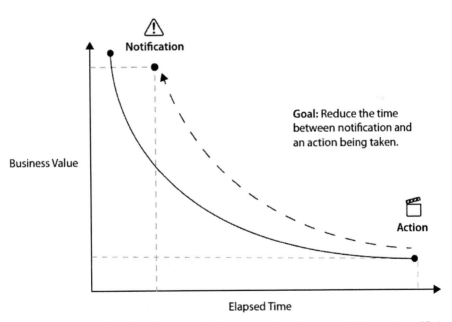

Figure 67: *The business value of notification and subsequent action decreases rapidly over time. SPA increases the speed of notification, and provides the necessary context for workers to take action as quickly as possible.*

Sidebar: Integrate the Internet of Things

The Internet of Things is the networked interconnection of everyday machines to one another, as well as to humans. Tiny sensors and actuators are proliferating at astounding speed, potentially linking 50 billion physical entities to make up the Internet of Things. This will affect many industries in many ways and will become a critical component of many organizations' Customer Company strategy.

Once a "thing" starts communicating through the Internet, the next step is to recognize the signals it sends and initiate a process to properly handle it. **Things, therefore, become participants in process applications, on the same level as a human**. They, too, can initiate steps, approve or reject requests, or be the target of process actions.

Businesses are therefore going to need to link the core processes, people and the plethora of sensors and devices to deliver true process excellence.

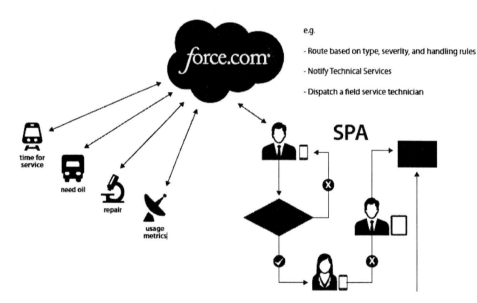

Figure 68: Things become SPA participants. Steps involving things become a dynamic repository of information about that thing.

Using SPA to manage the Internet of Things ensures that you don't bury the notification, decision making, routing and process initiation in the bowels of some application that users have no access to. SPA is able to monitor events and automatically trigger actions or initiate processes. It is able to make intelligent decisions about what to do with the incoming signals.

Accelerate the adoption of Force.com with SPA

We must learn to cocreate the future and use an improvisational model for strategy that embraces uncertainty, emerges from execution, engages individual creativity and learns by testing many hypotheses.
- Mike Rollings (Gartner), *Citizen Development: Reinventing the Shadows of IT*

For most companies, adopting a new "platform" is a major endeavor, consuming many hours of investigation, piloting, training, approvals and budgets.

This is a major inhibitor to getting Force.com implemented at all, never mind across the entire organization, which is when the power of the platform really kicks in.

The solution is to introduce SPA on the Force.com platform to the organization, and allow anyone to try it out. There is no training required, no major commitments to be made, and the results are immediate.

Lead with SPA

People will bypass and reject any system that does not help them perform work in a natural way.
- Gerhard Basson, Process Architect, Old Mutual (South Africa)

A Force.com SPA Builder distills the essence of Force.com into a format that is easily understandable to a knowledge worker with no technical background.

It is much easier for businesspeople to grasp and harness the power of Force.com when it is presented with SPA.

Force.com	SPA
Difficult for Excel/Access/Lotus users to make the connection to Force.com	Excel/Access/Lotus users don't need to make the connection to Force.com
Aimed primarily at IT	Aimed at any user or group
It's a major commitment to select a platform	It's simple to start using SPA
Need to find a suitable pilot project	No need for a pilot
Requires budget	Cost is inconsequential
Requires training	No training needed
Requires analysts and developers	Anyone can use it
It takes time to see the benefit	Get immediate benefit

Address resistance

People don't resist change. They resist being changed.
– Peter Senge, *The Fifth Discipline: The art and practice of the learning organization*

As succinctly put by Ian James[16]:

> *One thing you can count on – any attempt to ask a knowledge worker to reduce their jobs to a set of rote tasks that can be plugged into a new system is not going to work. Instead, many will be thinking, "I'm not going to tell him what I do when this happens, or that. I don't want any new system anyway."*

Cultural resistance tends to be a "bottom-up" phenomenon that occurs when people in individual work groups sabotage improvement efforts.

Whenever management decides to map a company's processes, your most creative employees may suspect you're measuring them for a straitjacket. They may feel the organization is threatening to take away their autonomy. They may become de-motivated or start looking for another job. They may even jump to a competitor who can see an unstructured process for what it really is: a pinball machine, not an assembly line.

In other words, the most creative people handling the most unstructured processes that add the most value to a company are most likely to resist any attempt to bring in traditional BPM software. After all, they've got the most to lose: their autonomy, initiative, and independent problem-solving skills.

On the other hand, most people will welcome SPA. After some initial suspicions, even the most valuable and creative people will likely realize the company is not trying to put them into a straitjacket, take away their autonomy, nor limit their decision making. On the contrary, the goal is to make everyone's jobs clearer and easier.

---

[16] Ian James, The Process Consultant

Leverage the network effect

The value of a tool that everyone can use comes when everyone uses it... for a thousand little things.
– Ian James, The Process Consultant

For an organization to be successful with SPA, it is not enough to simply build processes here and there. That alone will not turn a business into a more resilient, intelligent, fast, and flexible Customer Company.

To be successful, it is not good enough to be agile in one department but unable to link together operations in various parts of the business. If an innovation in the sales process means a product can't be shipped to the customer as quickly, then innovation, no matter how good locally, is not working for the business as a whole.

The vast majority of business value comes from the cumulative value of automating a large number of small workflow processes (currently likely to be run by Excel + email), and by having everyone in the organization on the same platform networking and sharing information with one another.

Return on Smart Process Application Implementations

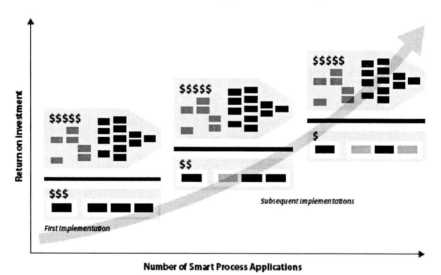

Figure 69: Seed SPA across the organization in order to capitalize on the network effect. The utility of SPA increases exponentially with the number of individuals using it.

Avoid the big bang approach

The citizen developer sits on the front lines of experimentation and business innovation. The innovation sought is not solely big-bang innovation, but all types of innovation that happen within the flow of business execution.

- Mike Rollings (Gartner), *Citizen Development: Reinventing the Shadows of IT*

Making a decision on adopting a new platform is momentous for most organizations and requires a major corporate initiative.

But SPA makes it easy for organizations to quickly take advantage of the Force.com platform anywhere in the organization at any time, with low risk and low cost. Any business unit can start small, with just a handful of processes. As others start seeing the benefits, and as the self-service database grows, they will join in.

Make it easy for workers to adopt

It is possible to set up organizations so that when I am pursuing my own self-interest, I automatically benefit everyone else, whether I mean to or not.
– Abraham Maslow

People naturally do what is in their own best interest, even if it negatively impacts the organization. You have to provide incentive so that the thing they do for themselves is in the best interest of the organization.

 The natural tendency will be for employees to want to stick to what they know. Therefore, you need to entice employees to adopt SPA for their everyday work. There is only one sure way to make users do this – make it so overwhelmingly attractive that they would only be hurting themselves if they used anything else.

Creating the conditions to facilitate quick adoption include:

- Establishing a Rapid Response Center early, to help users feel confident that support is available as they move forward.

- Making available a self-service database, which will make starting new solutions much faster.

- Creating a community group of SPA users to provide crowd-sourced support.

- Giving business units the ability to access and add their data to the SPA database, which will reduce the desire to access other data sources.

Seed the gurus

If you don't like change, you're going to like irrelevance even less.
- General Shinseki

Because change is so constant and so critical, without continual learning and sharing, today's guru will become tomorrow's loser.

Probably the most critical action to be taken is to turn yesterday's gurus into today's evangelists. Employees who are experts in the current tools being used, like Lotus Notes and Access, are likely to feel threatened by the advent of new technology. Seek these employees out and turn them into Force.com experts as early as possible. This way, instead of feeling threatened, they can use their expert status in yesterday's tools to become Force.com evangelists.

The rest will come. They trust the gurus and don't want to get left behind.

Just do it!

They always say time changes things, but you actually have to change them yourself.
- Andy Warhol

Don't wait for the Enterprise database to be built before starting to build applications. Instead, have the Enterprise database emerge as new applications are built and existing ones migrated.

With SPA, you don't have to get a solution completely right or get everything inputted in order to start getting value. Which is just as well, since perfect knowledge is impossible, and adjustments and improvements always need to be made after a solution is implemented.

Users of the SPA don't even have to know about it – things will just start showing up in their activity stream or email.

Conclusion

A more conservative wait-and-see approach can backfire by prolonging implementation and time to value, putting organizations at risk of losing face — or worse, business — to more proactive and aggressive competitors.
- Cognizant, *Mobilizing the enterprise*

We started out by looking at the challenges that face an organization on its journey to becoming a Customer Company.

As this book has shown, a well-implemented SPA solution can address many of these challenges by:

1. **Transforming your business processes** to provide the agility, customizability and adaptability required to meet the expectations of your customers.

2. **Facilitating an extended organization** to support efficient outsourcing, manage globalization and implement virtual business networks.

3. **Orchestrating the small slices of highly integrated, customized mobile applications** into complete, end-to-end processes.

4. **Contextualizing your social network** so that it becomes the default work console for your workers.

5. **Unlocking your legacy systems** without going through the costly and time-consuming effort to migrate them.

6. **Empowering knowledge workers to build their own solutions,** thereby tapping into the ability of Millennials to accomplish many things previously reserved for technical employees.

7. **Addressing the dangers of Shadow IT 2.0** by making SPA the easiest way for workers to build their own solutions, thereby reducing the risk of having to deal with multiple, often-duplicated toolsets and dispersed, unsecure data.

8. **Integrating the Internet of Things** by providing a way to make them part of your processes.

Smart process applications are inevitable. Every organization needs to address, in the words of Forrester, business activities that are people-intensive, highly variable, loosely structured, and subject to frequent change.

Empowering individuals and teams to take responsibility for building solutions with SPA will produce the flywheel affect – each small push, taken together over time, can have an enormous impact.

Imagine the level of innovation that can be achieved by enabling your employees to create applications that help them solve problems or take advantage of new business opportunities. Indeed, SPA represents billions of dollars in potential productivity gains, higher customer satisfaction, new business opportunities, faster time to market and more innovation.

With SPA, you are able to set your employees free. The result will be a peak-performing, robust and sustainable organization based on the shared efforts of thoroughly empowered, energized, self-reliant employees – in service of your Customer Company.

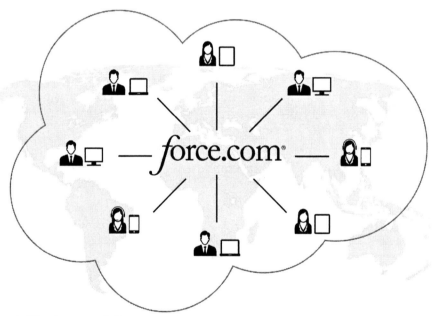

Figure 70: The ultimate goal: Everyone in the extended enterprise on the same business operations platform, regardless of the number and type of underlying system, using SPA as the business operation solution platform.

Appendix 1: Work-Relay

Simplicity is a great virtue but it requires hard work to achieve it and education to appreciate it. And to make matters worse: complexity sells better.
- Edsger Dijkstra, *The threats to computing science*

Work-Relay is elegantly simple yet powerful. Work-Relay provides an enormous amount of functionality in a well-designed interface that allows us to quickly build and adapt business process solutions to meet the ever-changing needs of our clients."
- Michaella Harkey, SVP, ExpertPlanet

Work-Relay is a SPA Builder that works on the Force.com platform. It is built on the ideas presented in this book.

For more information, visit **work-relay.com**

Appendix 2: Case Studies

The following case studies provide two different perspectives on SPA.

The first looks at SPA from the perspective of an implementation project that requires both process and time.

The second looks at SPA from the perspective of a typical process application.

Project-centric SPA

Background

A fast food company needs to implement a new point-of-sale system in all of their 6,000+ stores.

Scenario

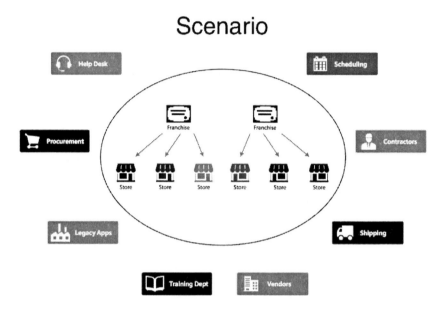

Figure 71: The solution needs to coordinate hundreds of franchises, thousands of stores, and a multitude of collaborating participants to successfully complete each implementation.

The number of tasks to be scheduled and tracked is extensive, from coordinating multiple vendors and contractors, ordering and shipping equipment, training employees and integrating the help desk. Some tasks can occur in parallel, while other tasks are interrelated and need to follow a specific sequence. All tasks are deadline-related, and if one step gets held up, it puts all other steps in the process on hold – even those steps that could be completed independently of the currently stalled step.

Previous Solution

The management of the point-of-sale integration project started out as a single spreadsheet and rapidly grew into a hodgepodge of many interrelated spreadsheets that were emailed around for data entry, cut-and-pasted, manually consolidated, and otherwise used well beyond the intended capabilities. It included:

1. A Master Spreadsheet
    *   Contains 68 columns
    *   Pulls data from 15 different "input files" which are updated on a weekly or daily basis
    *   Input files are updated by different departments (IT, Help Desk, Training, Operations, HR, and others)

2. The Master Schedule is refreshed weekly
    *   Six "output" files pull data from master schedule
    *   One file is distributed internally and five files are separated and sent to the appropriate vendors

Problems

Typical problems included:

- Heavily reliance on email.
- Important information falling through the cracks.
- Redundant messages/notifications.
- Flooded inboxes.
- Redundant processes.
- Difficulty finding information in Excel.
- No checks and balances system for missing information prior to install.
- No easy way to provide an overview of the project's progress.
- Manual scheduling.
- Manual workflow management.
- No integration with other teams and departments.
- Error-prone and time-consuming cutting and pasting spreadsheets.
- Missed sending of notifications and updates.
- Slow speed of huge spreadsheets.
- No central repository of information.
- Need for backups and disaster recovery.

Solution: Work-Relay.com

The Work-Relay solution includes the following:

- A centralized database provides a single, non-redundant source of truth, eliminating the cutting and pasting of spreadsheets, and manages an unlimited amount of data.
- Automated monitoring provides complete visibility over the implantation process for all involved, and a dashboard provides a snapshot of current status.
- Workflow eliminates lag time between tasks, and ensures that nothing falls through the cracks.
- Automated notifications and updates reduces lag time and cycle time.
- Guaranteed performance and uptime.
- Automated integration.
- Eliminated need for backups and disaster recovery.
- Chatter allows all parties, both inside and outside the organization, to communicate in real-time, significantly reducing email traffic and speeding up problem resolution.
- Chatter allows a knowledge base to be built organically, reducing the time required for future installation.

- Mobile enablement allows technicians to complete checklists and register and assign issues immediately.
- Reporting and analytics are used to determine violations of SLA's, bottlenecks, and comparative performance among vendors.

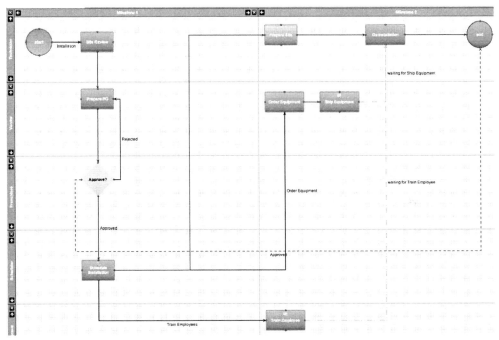

Figure 72: A stripped down view of the primary POS implementation business process.

Outcome

- A complete Work-Relay solution was built and deployed in six weeks.
- The solution effectively addressed all the problems identified above.
- No additional resources needed to be hired to complete the project in time.
- The project was completed six months earlier than planned.
- Beginning with 100+ users, it will eventually scale across the extended enterprise.

The future

With the execution of the point-of-sale management technology implementation project, the organization planted the seed for a comprehensive, enterprise-wide self-service database that can be used by anyone in the organization to build solutions for their needs. This has led to multiple departments taking advantage of the database and Work-Relay has been used to handle everything from change management to kitchen implement management.

As more users get on to the platform, the network effect has kicked in, and the company has been able to start using Chatter as an effective enterprise social network.

Process-centric SPA

Background

The requirement was to streamline the reaction of the organization to incidents on an oilrig utilizing mobile, social and cloud technology.

Requirements included:

- reporting an incident on a mobile device using a wizard pertaining to the type of incident that occurred;
- taking photos and videos and automatically uploading them with the report;
- depending on the type of incident, automatically notifying the appropriate people;
- recording of actions taken;
- triggering appropriate workflows;
- creating and assigning tasks;
- automatically generating the appropriate government forms;
- providing appropriate first aid instructions;
- taking into account the personal health records of the individuals being treated; and
- providing details of impending weather conditions that may impact incident recovery.

The solution also needed to:

- scale to accommodate a significant increase in usage and users in the case of, for example, a major oil spill;
- guarantee consistently fast performance;
- provide 99.99% uptime;
- provide pre-defined and ad hoc reports and dashboards;
- provide access to reports of similar incidents to see how they were dealt with, who was involved, and how to get hold of them;
- include a prearranged place to store documents related to the incident.

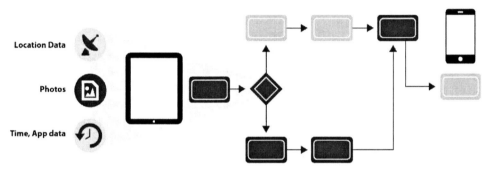

Figure 73: The information related to the incident needs to be recorded immediately using a mobile device, and trigger appropriate processes based on the type, severity and location of the incident.

Solution

Work-Relay allowed the application to be built with a minimal amount of code – the platform provided core functionality out-the-box, like security, authorization, roles and profiles; a relational database; mobile forms; workflows and wizards; and reports and dashboards.

Without Work-Relay, building the application would have required a technical architect to design the application architecture; a database administrator to design, implement and maintain the database; an analyst to write detailed functional specifications; a team of programmers to write code; a technical writer to ensure everything was well documented; and a project manager to coordinate the work of all personnel and all functions occurring within the application development process.

Common functionality for things like security and permissions, workflow, support for mobile devices, and much more, would need to be built into the application, as would less common but increasingly required functionality, such as support for multiple languages.

And writing the application is just one part of the equation. Add in the need to figure out what technology to use and how to integrate it, procure and implement the hardware and software, find and bring together the right team, plan scalability, ensure constant performance, implement backup and disaster recovery procedures – as a start. Then there is the need to make sure that the specifications are tight, because changing them later won't be easy.

Now, multiply this by all the applications your organization needs to build, and you begin to get a sense of how transformative Work-Relay can be.

With Work-Relay, the initial version of this application was up and running and deployed to thousands of users in a matter of a few weeks. This would not have been feasible without Work-Relay.

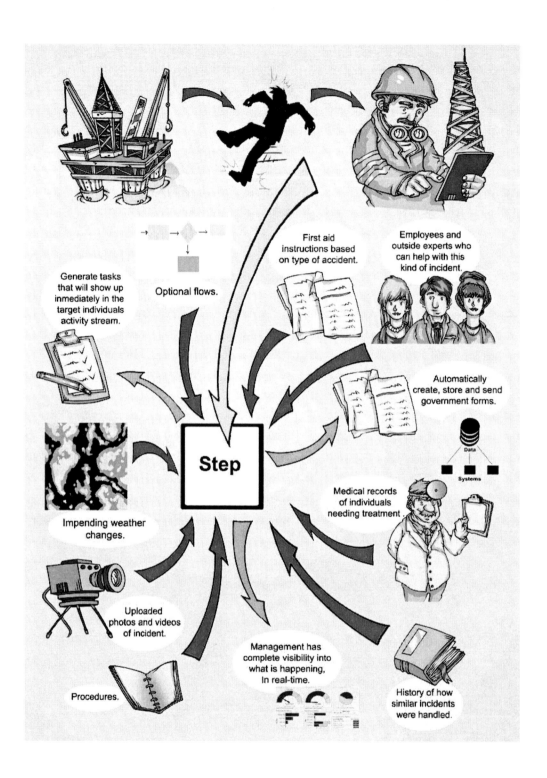

Appendix 3: Examples

Work-Relay can be used in any situation where multiple steps need to be taken by multiple people to reach a business objective.

 Processes that require tracking input from multiple people, as well as collaboration and approvals e.g. proposals, performance reviews

 Processes that follow both predefined and ad hoc steps e.g. insurance claim, property management

 Processes that require multiple steps in a predefined sequence e.g. permit applications, benefit enrollment

 Processes that are completely ad hoc based on unusual circumtances e.g. claims investigations, problem management

 Processes that require the collection of information before initiating specific action e.g. service requests, dispute management

 Processes that are long-running with periodic updates and actions e.g asset lifecycle management, policy renewals

 Processes initiated via alerts and routed to the appropriate people based on conditions e.g. medical alert management, change management

 Processes that coordinate the interrelated activities of many parties over an extended period of time e.g. equipment installation across many locations, construction projects

---

Finance
Purchase requisitions
Procurement activities
Capital appropriations
Accounts payable/receivable
Travel and expense

Procurement
Tender management
Vendor response collection and consolidation
Automatic, detailed procurement history for compliance and retrieval purposes

Government
License and permitting management
Service applications
Grant management
Benefit enrollment and qualification
Correspondence management

Telco
Asset lifecycle management
Complex onboarding process
Legal affairs management

Sales/CRM
Sales projections
Product specifications
Proposal generation
Customer care

Product launch
Product trial
Customer complaint management
Policy renewals

Education
Curriculum change management
Policy management
Action tracking

IT governance/COBIT/ITIL
Authorization management
Configuration management
Problem management
Change management
Service level management

Banking
Loan origination
Dispute management
Incident and exception handling

Corporate Services	Human Resources
Service request	New employee onboarding
Change request	Performance reviews
Document routing and approval	Applicant rating
	Employee administration forms
Manufacturing	
Product specification	**Project Management**
Product Lifecycle Management	Project file and document management
Contract lifecycle	Team collaboration
Product changes	Project status tracking
ISO 9000 compliance	Automatic reminders, escalations and alerts
Energy and Utilities	**Healthcare**
Rate case management	Claims investigations
Permit applications	Patient admissions and discharge
Property management	Care coordination
Incident management	
	ISO 17799
OSHA compliance	Risk assessment and treatment
Sarbanes Oxley	System policy
Real-time procedure monitoring	Asset management
Complete audit trail	Compliance

Bibliography

Accenture. *Rising Use of Consumer Technology in the Workplace Forcing IT Departments to Respond, Accenture Research Finds. Accenture.com.* N.p., 12 Dec. 2011. Web. 21 Oct. 2013.

Changing the Game: Monthly Technology Briefs. Issue brief. Capgemini, 5 Nov. 2011. Web. 5 Aug. 2012.

Cheshire, Mark. "API 2.0: Potential to Radically Reshape Value Chains for Business Development in the Cloud." *Sand Hill.* N.p., 28 June 2011. Web. 21 Oct. 2013.

Coffee, Peter. "Refuting Cloud 'Lock-In': Zero, One, Too." Web log post. *The Cloudblog.* Salesforce, 18 Jan. 2012. Web. 3 May 2013.

Fingar, Peter. "The Business Process Platform in the Sky." Editorial. *BPTrends.* N.p., Mar. 2009. Web. 13 Feb. 2011.

Fingar, Peter. *Dot.cloud: The 21st Century Business Platform Built on Cloud Computing.* Tampa, FL: Meghan-Kiffer, 2009. Print.

Fingar, Peter. *Extreme Competition: Innovation and the Great 21st Century Business Reformation.* Tampa, FL: Meghan-Kiffer, 2006. Print.

Fischer, Layna, Keith D. Swenson, Nathaniel Palmer, Bruce Silver, and Thomas Koulopoulos. *Taming the Unpredictable: Real World Adaptive Case Management : Case Studies and Practical Guidance.* Lighthouse Point, FL: Future Strategies, 2011. Print.

Friedman, Thomas L. "Made in the World." Editorial. *The New York Times* 29 Jan. 2012, New York ed.: SR11. 28 Jan. 2012. Web. 21 Mar. 2013.

Gartner. *Gartner Estimates Global 'IT Debt' to Be $500 Billion This Year, with Potential to Grow to $1 Trillion by 2015. Gartner.com.* N.p., 23 Sept. 2010. Web. 23 Sept. 2011.

Gartner. *Gartner Reveals Top Predictions for IT Organizations and Users for 2012 and Beyond. Gartner.com.* N.p., 1 Dec. 2011. Web. 1 Jan. 2012.

Hagel, John, III, and John Seely Brown. "The Power of the Social Cloud." Web log post. *HBR Blog Network.* Harvard Business Review, 15 Oct. 2010. Web. 15 Mar. 2011.

Hinchcliffe, Dion. "Moving Beyond Systems of Record to Systems of Engagement." Web log post. *Dachisgroup.com.* N.p., 8 June 2011. Web. 12 May 2012.

Hinchcliffe, Don. "Dion Hinchcliffe's Next-Generation Enterprises." *Open APIs Mature Into a Next-Generation Business Model.* EbizQ, 2 Dec. 2009. Web. 21 Oct. 2013.

How to Become a Customer Company. N.p.: n.p., n.d. *Salesforce.* Salesforce. Web. 21 Oct. 2012.

Hugos, Michael H. *Business Agility: Sustainable Prosperity in a Relentlessly Competitive World.* Hoboken, NJ: Wiley, 2009. Print.

Informatica. *Informatica Chairman and CEO to Deliver Big Data Keynote at Pacific Crest Global Technology Leadership Forum. GlobeNewswire.* NASDAQ OMX Group, 3 Aug. 2011. Web. 15 Aug. 2011.

James, Ian. "The Process Consultant." *The Process Consultant.* N.p., n.d. Web. 21 Oct. 2013.

"Knowledge Is of Two Kinds: Samuel Johnson." *Knowledge Is of Two Kinds: Samuel Johnson.* N.p., n.d. Web. 21 Oct. 2013.

"KONE - Salesforce." *Salesforce*. N.p., n.d. Web. 21 Oct. 2013.

Lyons, Daniel. "Jeff Bezos on Amazon's Success." *Slate Magazine*. Newsweek, 24
    Dec. 2009. Web. 21 Oct. 2013.

Making the Shift to the Next-Generation Enterprise. Rep. Cognizant, Mar. 2012. Web.
    21 Oct. 2013.

Maoz, Michael. *Magic Quadrant for the CRM Customer Engagement Center*. Rep.
    no. G00251937. Gartner, 13 May 2013. Web. 17 Oct. 2013.

Maslow, Abraham H., Deborah C. Stephens, Gary Heil, and Abraham H.
    Maslow. *Maslow on Management*. New York: John Wiley, 1998. Print.

McGuire, Chris, Phil Choi, and Caroline Roth. *Force Platform Fundamentals an
    Introduction to Custom Application Development in the Cloud*. [S.l.]:
    Salesforce, 2008. Print.

Mulholland, Andy. "2012: The Year of Unstructured Technologies and Market
    Change." Web log post. *CTO Blog*. Capgemini, 16 Jan. 2012. Web. 21 Feb.
    2012.

Mulholland, Andy. "Ten Game-Changing Technology Shifts for 2012." Web log
    post. *CTO Blog*. Capgemini, 3 Jan. 2012. Web. 15 Mar. 2012.

Plummer, Daryl C., and Peter Middleton. *Predicts 2012: Four Forces Combine to
    Transform the IT Landscape*. Rep. no. G00228739. Stamford: Gartner, 2011.
    Print.

Rangaswami, JP. "Musing Gently about Improvisation, Permission and Forgiveness."
    Web log post. *Confusedofcalcutta.com*. N.p., 29 Jan. 2012. Web. 28 Feb.
    2012.

Rollings, Mike. *Citizen Development: Reinventing the Shadows of IT*. Rep. Gartner, 2

    Feb. 2012. Web. 21 Oct. 2013.

Schadler, Ted, Matthew Brown, and Heather Martyn. *Mobilize Your Collaboration*

    Strategy – An Information Workplace Report. Rep. Forrester Research, 13

    July 2011. Web. 1 Mar. 2012.

Tapping the Elusive Millennial Mindset. Rep. CIO Custom Solutions Group and

    Cognizant, n.d. Web. 21 July 2013.

Van De Ven, Andrew, Raghu Garud, Douglas Polley, and Sankaran

    Venkataraman. *The Innovation Journey*. New York: Oxford UP, 1999. Print.

Ventana Research. *Ventana Research Releases New Benchmark Research on*

    Spreadsheets for the Twenty-First Century. Ventana Research. N.p., 2 Jan.

    2013. Web. 28 Feb. 2013.

Wainewright, Phil. "From Fixed to Frictionless Enterprise." Web log post. *ZDNet*.

    N.p., 27 Oct. 2011. Web. 20 Apr. 2012.

Acknowledgements

This book is based largely on the ideas presented in various publications by Forrester analysts Connie Moore, Craig le Claire and Andrew Bartels. These ideas have proved enormously beneficial not only in writing this book, but also in providing direction for my organizations SPA builder, Work-Relay.

Work on this subject by Ian James, Sandy Kemsley, Nathaniel Palmer, Keith Swenson, Max Pucher, and Thomas Koulopoulos have helped hone the ideas presented in the book.

Thanks to Peter Coffee for contributing his always insightful thoughts to the Foreword.

Huge thanks to Jorie Braunold, who did a splendid job making sure that what I wrote actually made sense, and keeping me focused on getting the book finally done.

- Jonathan Sapir

The last word from Dilbert

About the Authors

Jonathan Sapir

Founder and CEO of SilverTree Systems

 **JONATHAN SAPIR** has over thirty years' experience helping clients leverage information technology to build their businesses. He is the founder and CEO of SilverTree Systems, Inc., a software development company with offices in Chicago, New York and Miami.

Jonathan has written five well-received books, including *Igniting the Phoenix: A New Vision for IT* in 2003, which foretold many of the ideas that have become reality, especially in the areas of enterprise social software, cloud computing, and self-service application development; and *Power in the Cloud: Using Cloud Computing to Build Information Systems at the Edge of Chaos* in 2008, which looks at building information systems in the context of complex adaptive systems theory. His more recent books focused on the Salesforce platform, including *Unleash the Power of Force.com*, *The Executives Guide to Force.com: Enabling Shadow IT and Citizen Developers in the Age of Cloud Computing*, and *The Quick Start Guide to Implementing Force.com: From pilot to enterprise-wide adoption*.

Peter Fingar

Internationally recognized expert on business strategy, globalization and business process management

 **PETER FINGAR,** Executive Partner in the business strategy firm, Meghan-Kiffer Research, is one of the industry's noted experts on business process management, and a practitioner with over forty years of hands-on experience at the intersection of business and technology.

As a former CIO and college professor, Peter is equally comfortable in the boardroom, the computer room or the classroom. Peter has taught graduate computing studies in the U.S. and abroad. He has held management, technical and advisory positions with GTE Data Services, American Software and Computer Services, Saudi Aramco, EC Cubed, the Technical Resource Connection division of Perot Systems and IBM Global Services.

Peter has developed technology transition plans for clients served by these companies, including GE, American Express, MasterCard and American Airlines-Sabre. In addition to numerous articles and professional papers, he is an author of twelve landmark books. Peter has delivered keynote talks and papers to professional conferences in America, Austria, Australia, Canada, China, The Netherlands, South Africa, Japan, United Arab Emirates, Saudi Arabia, Egypt, Bahrain, Germany, Britain, Italy and France. www.peterfingar.com

Peter Coffee

VP and Head of Platform Research at Salesforce

 **PETER COFFEE** is best known for his longtime role as a commentator for Ziff Davis, where he was most recently Technology Editor for eWEEK, until joining Salesforce in January 2007. He has over twenty years' experience in evaluating information technologies and practices as a developer, consultant, educator, and internationally published author and industry analyst.

Peter is the author of *Peter Coffee Teaches PCs*, published in 1998 by Que, and wrote Que's ZD Press tutorial *How to Program Java*.

Before joining eWEEK (then called *PC Week*) full-time in 1989, Peter held technical and management positions at Exxon and The Aerospace Corporation, dealing with chemical facility project control, Arctic project development, strategic defense analysis, end-user computing planning and support, and artificial intelligence applications research.